Prophet Shares God's Light

Cover Design by
bespokebookcovers.com

Copyright © 2015 F.U.N. Inc.
All rights reserved.
ISBN: 978-0-9962166-6-1

Prophet Shares God's Light

Del Hall and Del Hall IV

Nature Awareness School

Manifest Your Divine Nature

UPLIFT
WITH DREAMS

F.U.N. Inc.

Acknowledgments

It is with the deepest love and gratitude we thank all those who contributed to this book. Their willingness to share some of their sacred experiences made this book possible. These testimonies show that so much more is possible in your relationship with God. We hope that reading them will inspire you to more fully accept the Hand of the Divine.

The authors would also like to thank all those who helped in the editing of this book. Emily and Anthony Allred, Catherine and David Hughes, and Kate Hall. Your keen eyes and thoughtful suggestions made a huge difference in the telling of these profound stories.

"The days of any religion or path coming between me and my children are coming to an end" saith the Lord

December 29, 2013

Table of Contents

Section Two - Growing and Conditioning 103

Section Three - Traveling the Heavens 247

Foreword

We have all had hard times at one point or another. Whether it was from heartbreak, stress, the loss of a loved one, or some other cause. For me, it was a lack of meaning. Many years ago I found myself asking, "What's the point of all this? Isn't there more to life than the daily grind? Does any of this really matter at all?" One dark night the pain of this emptiness seemed overwhelming. I found myself face down on my bedroom floor, crying out for help. "Please, please, please!" The words tumbled out of my mouth, and tears fell down my face. I did not know what I was asking for, or to whom I was asking. But an answer came, nonetheless.

As I laid on the floor, a gentle shower of light began raining down upon me. It was subtle at first; invisible to the naked eye but as real as anything else in the room. I was surprised; I had never experienced anything like this! Soon the gentle shower grew into a mighty downpour, cascading into my bedroom. Although I could not see it, I knew this rain of light was as real as the walls, carpet, and furniture within arm's reach. As the rain touched my skin, the anguish inside of me was transformed into a gratitude and peace that I had never before known. My cries of "please, please, please!" were transformed into "thank you, thank you, thank you!" As the shower gradually faded, the peace lingered. The unhappiness was gone, but I had new questions in my heart: Where did this light come from? And how could I find it again?

Answers to these inquiries proved elusive. I had been to church many times, but had never heard of anything like this. It was unmistakably real, so why hadn't someone else told me that this was possible? I knew I'd had a real spiritual experience, but I did not know whom I could talk to about it. I wondered if anything like this would ever happen to me again. Years passed, but the memory remained. My thirst for truth grew greater, and my love for nature along with it. When the time was right, a trusted friend told me about the Nature Awareness School. Perhaps here I could find the answers I'd been seeking. I decided to enroll in a retreat.

During a guided spiritual experience at the retreat, this rain of light again showered down upon me. This time it was even more personal, more healing, more energizing, and deeper. The light poured in, filling every part of me with love, joy, and peace. It permeated and nourished my very being, Soul, the real me. Once again, the light had touched me like nothing else ever had. And this time, there was no question where it had come from: This was God's Light, sent from Him as a gift of love.

Finally, here were the answers I had been seeking. Del, the teacher, was able to tell me not only where this light came from, but how to connect with God's Love directly. He taught me certain spiritual tools that can help one draw closer to God, such as singing HU, the ancient love song to God, and an appreciation for the blessings that God puts into our lives each and every day. Del also taught me that by building a relationship with the current Prophet of God, one can be taught the ways of God directly. His teachings were like water for my thirsty spirit. He explained passages from the Bible in a way that made more sense than I had ever heard before; like he knew the teachings of Jesus at a deeper level than any priest or preacher. Over the next ten years, his teachings changed my life completely. I went from a life without purpose to a life of incredible abundance and joy.

I am one of the Prophet's students at the Nature Awareness School. Del has helped all of us achieve a life of greater meaning, built on individual experiences with the Divine. Now we are reaching out to share what we have been given. It is a view of life unlike any other – one based on true, personal experience with God's Love. Our books, "Testimonies of God's Love" books one and two, "Visiting Loved Ones in Heaven," and this book highlight a small fraction of the examples that we have witnessed over the years. Our hope is that these books will help the reader on his or her own spiritual path. That it will inspire many to climb the spiritual mountain, to seek truth, and to build or improve their own relationship with God and His Prophet.

God's Love is very real. Indeed it as real as the air we breathe, if not more real. It transcends all religions and paths. He reached out to me before I even knew his name, before I even knew where to look for Him. He knew what I needed, just when I needed it. He can do the same for you.

David Hughes

Student at Nature Awareness School since 2005

Preface

 This book was written to share beautiful and profound spiritual adventures with God's Light, made possible by God's Grace through His Prophet. The hope is to inspire the reader to invest more in their own personal relationship with God and that they too could grow spiritually towards having similar experiences. While these testimonies were being reviewed for this book it became apparent that sharing these profound spiritual experiences alone, without some background information, would produce an incomplete book. Without an introductory understanding of God's hand picked and Divinely trained Prophet, the testimonies would imply that a seeker can decide to go to God's Temples of learning or to the Abode of God uninvited and unprepared. Trying to do so would be infinitely more difficult than attempting to climb Mount Everest alone without a guide. One needs training and conditioning to withstand the unimaginable intensity of love when face to face with an aspect of God.

 God ALWAYS has a Prophet of His choice on

Earth.   Each of God's Prophets throughout history has a unique mission. One may only have a few students with the sole intent to keep God's teachings and truth alive. God may use another to change the course of history. God's Prophets are usually trained by both the current and former Prophets. The Prophet is tested and trained over a very long period of time. The earlier Prophets are physically gone but teach the new Prophet in the inner spiritual worlds. This serves two main purposes: the trainee becomes very adept at spiritual travel and gains wisdom from those in whose shoes he will someday walk. This is vital training because the Prophet is the one who must safely prepare and then take his students into the Heavens and back.

There are many levels of Heaven, also called planes or mansions. Saint Paul once claimed to know a man who went to the third Heaven. Actually it was Paul himself that went, but the pearl is, if there is a third Heaven, it presumes a first and second Heaven also exist. The first Heaven is often referred to as the astral plane. Even on just that one plane of existence there are over one hundred sub-planes. This Heaven is where most people go after passing from a physical body, unless they receive training while still here in their physical body. Without a guide who is trained properly in the ways of God a student could misunderstand the intended lesson and become confused as to what is truth. The inner worlds are enormous compared to the physical worlds. They are very real and can be explored safely when guided by God's Prophet.

Some of my students share experiences of when they were taken to God's Temples of learning, and even to the twelfth Heaven, the primary Abode of God. It is here, in these higher worlds, where students experience God's truths at a depth of knowingness beyond what is possible by only studying physical scripture alone. After reaching this level of spiritual experience, physical scripture will come alive with truth at new and higher levels. At this point one actually values scripture more than they could have possibly valued it before their own personal experience.

The primary message of this book is: God wants you to KNOW that you can truly have a more personal and loving relationship with the Divine. Your relationship with the Divine has the potential to be more profound, personal, and loving than any organized religion currently teaches on Earth. The Nature Awareness School is NOT a religion, it is a school. God and His Prophet are NOT disparaging of any religion of love. However, the more a path defines itself with its teachings, dogma, or tenets, the more "walls" it inadvertently creates between the seeker and God. Sometimes it even puts God into a smaller box. God does not fit in any box. The Prophet is for all Souls and is purposely not officially aligned with any path, but shows respect to all.

Part of my mission is to share more of what is spiritually possible for you as a child of God. Few Souls know or understand that God's Prophet can safely guide God's children, while still alive physically, to their Heavenly home. Taking a child of God into the Heavens is not the job of clergy. Clergy has a responsibility to pass on the teaching of their religion exactly as they were taught, not to add additional concepts or possibilities. If every clergy member taught their own personal belief system no religion could survive for long. Then the beautiful teachings of an earlier Prophet of God would be lost. Clergy can be creative in finding interesting and uplifting ways to share their teachings, but their job is to keep their religion intact. However, God sends His Prophets to build on the teachings of His past Prophets, to share God's Light, and to guide Souls to their Heavenly home.

There is ALWAYS MORE when it comes to God's teachings and truth. No one Prophet can teach ALL of God's ways. It may be that the audience of a particular time in history cannot absorb more wisdom. It could be due to a Prophet's limited time to teach and limited time in a physical body on Earth. Ultimately, it is that there is ALWAYS MORE! Each of God's Prophets brings additional teachings and opportunities for ways to draw closer to God, building on the work and teachings of former Prophets. That is one reason why Prophets of the past ask God to send another; to comfort, teach, and continue to help God's children grow into greater abundance. Former Prophets continue to have great love for God's children and want to see them continue to grow in accepting more of God's Love. One never needs to stop loving or accepting help from a past Prophet in order to grow with the help of the current Prophet. All true Prophets of God work together and help one another do God's work.

Del Hall III

Introduction

The all-creative Word of God flows eternally as a mighty river of spiritual light and spiritual sound. It lacks nothing. It originates at the Abode of God and travels down through the Heavens, all the while creating, sustaining, nurturing, purifying, and ultimately carrying Soul back home to God. This life force has been called many names throughout the course of history; the Holy Ghost, the Word, the Music of the Spheres, Divine Spirit, the Eck, the Essence of the Creator, the Force, Logos, and countless others. Whatever it is you prefer to call it, one thing remains constant - it is an expression of God's Love for us, and it is most certainly still available in this day and age. How sad to think that God no longer loves, communicates with, or blesses His children. God is a living God and He continues to rain down His Light and Love on His creation! It is vital to experience His Light if you seek to see through the illusions and distractions of the physical world and truly know God. For it is through His Light that God delivers the blessings of peace, joy, clarity, wisdom, healing, truth, higher consciousness, and so much more. All of these are gifts of love from a loving God, and are necessary if one desires to know more fully thy ways and thy truths.

It is this Light and Love of God that animates you and me - the real you and me, Soul. A Soul is not something you "have;" you "are" Soul. You are an eternal spiritual being within a temporal physical embodiment. When the body comes to its end the real you, Soul, will continue on. Not only does God's Light animate Soul, Soul is actually made of this Light. In essence, Soul is an individualized piece of the Holy Spirit. We are not God, nor will we ever become God, but in a very real sense we are, as Soul, a piece of the Voice of God. This is the true meaning behind the statement of being created in the image of God.

The Voice of God, or the Holy Spirit, is singular, but it manifests as spiritual light and spiritual sound. Most of the world is familiar with the idea of spiritual light but fewer know about spiritual sound. For it is upon the returning wave of sound that Soul travels Home to the Heart of God. To Soul this is simple. However, man and the mind of man are easily blinded to Soul's

Divinity. We become so caught up in the "passing parade" of life that it becomes hard for Soul to hear above the noise of the mind. Many begin to identify more with their physical selves and forget they are a child of God. It becomes harder and harder for them to recognize their Divinity.

This is why God sends mankind His Prophets. We need someone who sees clearly and can gently blow away the fog that is obscuring our vision. Someone who can help us soar free as spiritual eagles. We need someone to teach us the "Language of the Divine" so that we may recognize and understand the Divine guidance available for us. We need a living teacher who can prepare us and teach us thy ways and thy truth in both the waking and dream states. We need a guide who is authorized to take us on journeys into the Heavens to gain in wisdom and ultimately meet our maker – while still living in a physical body. We need someone who is authorized to pass on God's Light and Love so that we may be purified, uplifted, and benefit from the multitude of blessings contained within His Light. Mankind is never without a Prophet – we are never alone. This is the greatest proof of God's Love for man – a continuous unbroken chain of Divinely chosen and trained Prophets sent to show us the way home.

In his role as the Light Giver my father, the current Prophet, has been authorized to share God's Light and Love with his students. Although this book contains many pearls of wisdom this is the core focus of this script - experiences with the Light and Sound of God. Testimonies are loosely grouped into three sections, although there is some overlap. Contained within the first section are experiences where seekers are ever so gently awakened to God's Light. Their spiritual eye begins to be opened and the seeker realizes there is more to life. In the second section are testimonies where the Prophet conditions his students to God's Light and helps them remove mental blocks to continue growth – such as fear, worry, anger, vanity, and excessive attachments. In the third section, after building even more trust with the Prophet and becoming very comfortable with God's Light and with spiritual travel, students are taken to spiritual temples within the various Heavens. Some are even led Home to the Abode of God. It is through this teaching method of direct personal experience that Soul can most benefit. We

4

believe you will understand more from this book by reading the sections in order.

It is with great humility, reverence, and love that the authors share these experiences, blessings, and insights with you. They know that God is truly reaching out through His Prophet to develop a more personal and loving relationship with each and every one of us. They know that you too can experience even greater joy and abundance in your life by experiencing the Light and Love of God.

Del Hall IV

HU – A Love Song to God

All the authors who contributed to this book sing HU daily. Many of their amazing experiences are a direct result of tuning in and opening their hearts through this spiritual practice.

HU is an ancient name for God that can be sung quietly or aloud in prayer. HU has existed since the beginning of time in one form or another and is available to all regardless of religion. It is a pure way to express your love to God and give thanks for your blessings.

Singing HU (HUUUUUU pronounced hue) serves as a tuning fork with Spirit that brings you into greater harmony with the Divine. We recommend singing HU a few minutes each day. This can bring love, joy, peace, and clarity, or help you rise to a higher view of a situation when upset or fearful.

Section One

Section One

Awakening to the Light

The focus of this book is to share actual experiences my students had with God's Light or Sound. God's Light and Sound are both aspects of the Voice of God and are similar in that they are both vibrations. Generally one experiences the Light of God first and later, after more training, the Sound of God. Student testimonies in this section share first-time or early experiences with the Light or Sound of God, which is the Holy Spirit. The Holy Spirit comes in many forms and can be consciously perceived by inner nudges, knowingness, feelings of peace, clarity, dreams, and spiritual Light or Sound.

Having conscious experiences with God's Light is vital for any serious student of God's teachings. Many blessings are received when in the presence of God's Light. God's Light contains love that manifests in a multitude of different forms. This love can manifest as peace, joy, clarity, healings, spiritual truth, increased trust in the Prophet's Divine authority, and more. This is why God has always given His true Prophet, throughout all of history, the authority to share the Light of God with others. These gifts of love are delivered in the perfect dose for each individual. In the beginning the light and love is subtle, almost unrecognizable. However, once the individual is spiritually strengthened the intensity and receptiveness of the blessings increase greatly.

As God's Prophet, I take great care not to overwhelm a new seeker with too much light and love during the first few retreats at the school. Too much light given too quickly can cause a new seeker to lose balance, unintentionally slowing their spiritual growth. I listen to and precisely follow God's will for each individual. I hope you can gather from these testimonies how exciting it is to witness God's Light for the first time. As the Prophet it is such a joy to see the beautiful transformation that the Light of God creates in an individual.

1

God's Gentle White Light Transforms Me

Many times our initial experiences with the Light of God can be subtle. If we receive too much too fast it can put us out of balance. It takes time to acclimate to more and more intense experiences with the Light and Love of God. God and His Prophet know exactly what is appropriate for each individual.

I was a seeker. I traveled the world looking for a path home to God. I tried going to church with friends. I tried yoga and dance. I tried fasting and strict diets. I tried meditation retreats. None of these left me feeling any closer to God. Having seen nothing, having no lasting peace, and no lasting joy to speak of. During one of the first classes I took at the Nature Awareness School many years ago, I received a vision of God's gentle white Light. In a moment this experience awakened something in me that I did not even know was sleeping; a yearning to experience more of God's Love and a desire to be able to communicate with the Divine.

Our teacher had instructed us to find a comfortable place to sit in the woods, and to relax. We were told we might experience something new, see the beauty of the woods or an animal moving. But the key was to just relax. "Unplug" and just be. While I have loved hiking in nature since I was a little child, just relaxing in it was new to me. So I found a suitable rock, got comfortable, watched the wind blow the trees, and listened to the creek flow by. I saw a chipmunk dart here and then there. I just relaxed and enjoyed the woods. Then I saw a gentle white light appear like a cloud in front of me. My eyes were open, yet the light I was seeing was not physical light. As I tried to look closer at what it was, it disappeared; but a presence of peacefulness remained. What was it that I had seen? I felt lighter and freer, and walked back into the class with a little more bounce in my step.

When we returned to class students started sharing their experiences. Del explained that Divine Spirit has many ways of expressing Itself to us, but one of the most direct ways is through the Light of God. God had been communicating with me when I sat on that rock. Wow, was I blessed! I had finally found what I had been looking for.

Since then, especially at retreats, but also at home using the tools Del taught me, the Light of God has revealed Itself to me. Each experience with God's Light has transformed me slightly - has left me with a little more peace, a little more confidence, a little more joy, a little more freedom. Sometimes I have asked myself "why me?" I am an ordinary person, not a saint like I had read about in the Bible. I am a wife and a mom. I thought only special people or saints could have heavenly visions.

Yet because God loves us, He showers His blessings on us. I consider myself to be extremely blessed to have a living teacher that can help me to not only have these experiences, but to understand the message. He shows me how to integrate the peace and love and freedom into my daily life. I am a living testimony that seeing God's Light changes us. It is the love that I received in these experiences that changed me. Where I used to be fearful, now I trust. Where I used to have a kind of sour attitude toward life, now I am truly happy. The

Light of God nurtured me and transformed me from the inside out.

The Nature Awareness School is on a beautiful piece of land, but even more than the physical beauty is the opportunity to be in the presence of a true Prophet of God. Here in a seemingly simple exercise of sitting in the woods, I saw the Light of God. There is something special about the opportunity to attend one of Del's classes. I have witnessed many people experience the Light of God during his retreats. Maybe Heaven will open a doorway for you to look through too.

God is still alive and still wants to bless us. He is just as amazing as He was thousands of years ago, and the Holy Spirit still reveals Itself to us through Light. I believe He wants to see all of us walk a little lighter, to see us all live with more peace, joy, and freedom. For us to receive His reassurance, that no matter who we are or where we are in our lives, he cares. He truly loves us.

Written by Molly Comfort

2

Finding the Light of God

God is a living God and wants to communicate with His children. How sad, ridiculous really, to believe God no longer communicates with His children. When one experiences God's Light, it is a form of communication and a gift of love. The following is a heartfelt testimony to seeing the Light of God for the first time and the gratitude that followed.

I recall with great clarity one of my first experiences with the Light of God in this lifetime. In the 1990's I took a break from my college engineering studies to attend a retreat at the Nature Awareness School. At this retreat, I was introduced to a sacred sound, which is both an ancient name for God and a love song to God. This sound is written as HU.

We had been singing HU for a while with our teacher and I became aware of a blue light gently filling the space around me. After a while I also saw a brilliant white light shining into my consciousness. It mattered not if my eyes were open or closed. I could see the light as clearly as the sun on a summer day. Surprised as I was to see this light, I was not afraid, but excited to see this proof that there is much more to life than what our physical senses perceive. A great sense of deep peace descended upon me as I saw the light grow stronger as we continued to sing HU.

Sometime after the experience, I took time on my own to kneel quietly in the woods and reflect on what I had experienced. In that moment, for the first time in this life, I knew that God is real and that God loves us. I once believed that experiencing the Light of God would be an ultimate experience, the pinnacle of a lifetime. Yet this is not so. This experience, as profound a blessing as it was, was simply my first step on a journey, like a child's first splash in a wading pool. God wants to bless you. Look for God's Light, and begin your own active relationship with God and God's Prophets.

Written by Timothy Donley

3

The Blue Light of God

The Light of God manifests itself in many different colors. Each color has a specific meaning and can provide additional insight into the nature of your experience. To witness any aspect of the Light of God is a profound blessing and an expression of God's Love for you.

Before I attended my first class at the Nature Awareness School I had come across references to spiritual light in books and heard people talk about it, but this light was nonetheless a mental concept to me. It was something that I had no personal experience with.

All of this changed during my first class at the school. I was sitting out in the woods one evening as part of an awareness exercise when a beautiful deer walked in front of me. It was alerted by a slight turn of my head and started snorting and moving its head back and forth as it tried to identify me amid the fading light of day.

My heart went out to the deer, as I felt love for this part of God's creation, when suddenly everything in my field of vision - the deer, the trees, everything around me - became filled with a shimmering blue light. During this I felt Divine Love flood into my heart and fill my whole being.

The deer then bounded off and I stood up, amazed by what had just taken place. I had the knowing in my heart that Divine Spirit is real, and that what I had just experienced was way beyond anything that I could ever perceive with my physical senses alone. When I shared this experience with Del he did not seem at all surprised. He said that it was great and an important step on my path, and that there is a lot of spiritual help available to me. This experience was so stunning to me that I felt compelled to return to the school for a spiritual retreat and learn more about this amazing blue light.

As I attended more classes and continued to have more experiences with the blue light, both on and off of the school property, in dreams and while awake, I came to learn that this light was one of the aspects of the Light of God. It was also the calling card of my inner spiritual guide and teacher, the one who is a true Prophet of God. This beautiful blue light has been a

20

constant companion to me over the twenty years that have passed since that unforgettable summer evening at the Nature Awareness School.

Sometimes it comes as a flash of light so small that I could easily miss it if I was not paying attention. Whenever I see it, it is a welcome reminder that my guide and teacher is spiritually with me. This presence helps me to make better choices that have led to a life of an abundance of peace, love, and the strength to endure life's challenges. This is an abundance that I never dreamed was possible twenty years ago when all that I could see was filled with the blue Light of God. I am grateful to Del and the Nature Awareness School for creating a peaceful, relaxed setting, away from the stresses of daily life in which to experience God's Love and Its Light, a light that has within it everything that I need.

Written By Roland Vonder Muhll

4

He Held My Hand

*The HU Song is one of the greatest gifts we could pass
on to you. Singing HU will strengthen your connection
to Spirit regardless of what path you are on. Singing HU
will raise you up and open you up. Many of the
phenomenal experiences with the Light of God
occurred, in part, due to singing HU.*

Back in August I went to a HU sing at the
Nature Awareness School. HU is a love song to
God. There were about 80 people there, a lot
whom I have never met before. Del, the Prophet
of God, came in and explained the song and
where it originated. Then he began to sing HU
and everyone followed.

The sound of everyone singing HU was just so
beautiful; it was the most people I have ever
sung with. As we were singing I became very
relaxed. With my eyes closed, as I continued
singing, I started to see these small lights. Some
were blue and some were white. Then I saw a

door, and in the door was a rectangle of bright white light shining through. Being somewhat new to this experience, I could feel myself get anxious and the door was gone.

I sat back, relaxed and continued to sing HU. The door with the white light appeared again. I stayed relaxed, then I felt a hand take mine and we walked to the door. I did not feel any anxiety or nervousness this time. We walked to the door and it opened. Inside was the brightest white light I have ever seen; it just filled the area.

Standing in the doorway and still holding the Prophet's hands, I began absorbing this beautiful white light. It was warm, but more than that I felt this overwhelming presence of peace. We just stood there and never said a word.

When I sing HU at home, I thank God for giving me such an experience that I can visit over and over again.

Written by Steven Lane

5

I Am Not Alone – The First Time I Experienced God's Light

God is a living God. As uplifting as scripture can be it seems a shame to think God only spoke to His children in the past. I am confident God is alive and well. He still loves us and communicates with us in this day and age. One of the many ways the Divine can communicate to us is with spiritual light. The following is a beautiful story about seeing the Light of God for the first time. What a blessing!

In 1995 I was living in California, but was working here in Virginia for a one-year temporary job-assignment. I was in a searching and seeking phase of my life – though not sure what I was looking for. It was an unsettled time, lots of change in several areas of my life. I had no real direction or rooting in anything or anywhere it seemed. I saw a small advertisement in a local magazine for the Nature Awareness School. I was immediately interested and called and spoke to Del on the phone. I can remember our conversation like it was yesterday. We talked about various things and the types of classes he was teaching, but it was something in his voice that spoke to me on a deeper level. I knew I wanted to go no matter what the next class was. Back then the school offered a mix of wilderness skills and spiritual retreats and it turned out the next class was a tracking class. Driving up to the school alone and taking this class was a whole new experience for me, as I had never done anything like this before but I was excited to go. I was open to learn and to whatever adventure was in store. I enjoyed the class and found I had a natural ability to see the tracks in the dirt during our practice sessions.

While there I was more relaxed and at peace than I could ever recall. At the time I was afraid of the dark and being in the woods at night, but not as much here. I felt safe and protected and knew I was in good hands. I slept like a baby. One night after class was over and everyone had gone to bed I stood on the grassy hill overlooking the pond. I was soaking in the beauty of the clear sky and the brilliant stars, appreciating the calmness and grateful for the courage I had to stand there "alone" in the dark and still be at peace.

I became aware of a bright white light over my right shoulder just out of my peripheral vision. It surprised me but it was a gentle presence that did not scare me. I turned quickly to see it but when I looked it was gone. I eventually settled down and went back to looking out over the pond, enjoying the peacefulness, and saw the white light once again. This time I turned slowly hoping to see more of the light and what it was; but as I turned around enough to look directly, it was gone again. This happened again, but this time I did not turn at all and used wide-angle vision we were taught in class to observe and be aware of the light without looking directly at it. It was comforting, gentle, and non-intrusive yet it seemed to hold so much more. I was not sure what it was, but I liked it and I knew I was not alone.

The next day I mentioned my experience to Del and he helped me understand that what I was seeing was the Light of God. Divine Spirit can come in many forms and one is light. Later I would learn that this presence is always with me whether I see it or not. Out of great love for me though, it chose to introduce Itself in a way that would not scare me. It was, as I learned in later spiritual retreats, offering to have an inner personal relationship and help guide me spiritually. In time, by nurturing this relationship, by singing HU, and being grateful for its blessings, this relationship has grown in trust and a true love connection has developed.

Almost twenty years later, as I sit writing this story in the same spot on the grassy hillside looking out at the pond, I am filled with appreciation, love, and awe at how every aspect of my life has been transformed because of this very real, very present, and very personal relationship with Divine Spirit. In the past twenty years I've gone through zigs and zags, and ups and downs in life, had relationship changes, career and finance changes, and relocations of homes, but the one constant has been this ever-growing love connection. It is the solid foundation upon which my life rests and is a source of peace, stability, comfort, joy, and happiness even on some of the more difficult days. I am truly never alone. What a magnificent discovery and journey this has been and continues to be

Written by Lorraine Fortier

6

An Awakening

*We can experience the Light of God in the waking state
or, like in the following example, the dream state.
Either way, our initial experiences with the Light are
often to "wake us up" from our slumber and inspire us
to make the journey home to God. It is the Love of God
that draws us home.*

A little over ten years ago I attended my first class at the Nature Awareness School called "Wild Edible Plant Weekend." I did not know at the time how much this choice would transform my life in beautiful abundant ways. All I knew was that I was looking forward to spending a weekend in the mountains away from the everyday humdrum of city life. Upon arrival I felt something special about this place. Peace had entered my heart and I enjoyed the beauty that surrounded me. On the surface this was just a wild edible plant class, but I felt something deeply spiritual stir within me that weekend.

After the class I had a vivid dream of flying down the gravel road that leads to the school. I saw Del, who I now know is a true Prophet of God, and his wife Lynne, sitting on a bench outside their home. As I flew towards them they stood up and I saw beautiful white light shine around them. The light was stunning and would have been too much for human eyes, but through the eyes of Soul I found this light welcoming and nurturing. I said, "I don't know why I am here?" and they replied, "Well, we are glad that you came." This was the Light of God shining through them to me and the love, Divine Love, I felt flowing from them awakened the true me, Soul, a Divine spark of God.

This dream was a gift of love from God through His Prophet to help me "wake up" spiritually. The spiritual tools that Del has taught me for the past ten years have allowed me to accept my Divinity as Soul, and make God a reality in my life. This precious and sacred gift of knowing from experience that my Heavenly Father loves me and has sent His Prophet to show me my way Home is something that I cannot keep to myself. My heart sings to be an instrument of God to give and receive Divine Love so other Souls, like you perhaps, may awaken to your Divine nature as well and truly know God loves you and that His Prophet is here to help show you your way Home.

Written by Shanna Canine

7

My First Time With the Light

It is a special moment when Soul first consciously experiences the Light of God. The Light can manifest itself in many different ways but the message contained within is consistent. "God loves you and you are not alone!" As students are blessed to repeatedly experience the Light of God in Its many forms they become more acclimated to being it Its presence. They can now accept even greater amounts of peace, joy, clarity, love, guidance, and truth.

My first experience with seeing the Light of God came during a spiritual retreat at the Nature Awareness School in October 2000. I had been taught the HU the year before. Occasionally during that earlier weekend, Del would invite us to take an old blanket and go find a place to sit alone either in the woods or by the pond or on a rock. After settling in to our surroundings, we would close our eyes, focus on the area behind and slightly above eye level, and reverently sing HU, an ancient name for God. He explained that when sung with a grateful heart and as a love song to God, this vibration tunes us in to the realms beyond what our physical senses can detect. It begins to wake up our spiritual senses, and at the same time helps heighten even our physical senses to be able to perceive more of what is around us, a very valuable survival skill.

This time we stayed in the building and sang HU in a group for a few minutes, then sat quietly afterward with our eyes still closed to watch, listen, and receive. In that relaxed receptive state I saw with my eyes closed, lots of blue dots, then yellow, and streaks of white light. Then I saw waves of blue light fly up and out like doves ascending right through the ceiling. I felt a deep sense of gratitude and love, like I was being invited to "fly" with Spirit. I was shown more yellow, blue, and white lights, and then green light in abstract patterns. I am so grateful for this gift from God, it was like God was saying, "Hello, I love you" and took me for a tour of the Heavenly realms and back! I learned that the colors indicate which state of consciousness one is being lifted up to, for a glimpse of what it would be like to dwell there. I had heard people say many times "God loves you" and "Love lifts you up." This time I experienced these truths personally!

Since then I have been given many, many inner experiences with the Light and Sound of God, each tailor made for what I needed at that time in my spiritual growth. These experiences have lifted my perspective and given me insights and clarity to make better decisions in life about everything from daily activities to major career changes. I now know the Light and Sound of God dwells within and all around us all the time, whether we are aware of it or not. We are never alone. Thank you God!

Written by Paul Sandman

8

Thankful I Shared

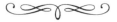

*The greatest hindrance to accepting our initial
experiences with the Light and Sound of God can
sometimes be ourselves. We let our mind, which is
fearful of change, cause us to doubt. It is during times
like these when it is key to have a teacher who
understands the "Language of the Divine."*

During my first three day spiritual retreat at
the Nature Awareness School, Del encouraged
us to participate in a relaxing sit exercise. During
this sit exercise we were instructed to go find a
place to sit outside, relax, and enjoy being in the
mountains. I found a spot in the woods on a
large smooth rock. After I got comfortable, I
began to think of something I was grateful for to
help open my heart. I then sang HU for a while.
When I was done singing HU, I asked the
Prophet to show me Divine Love. I looked
around at my lush green oasis in the woods. I felt
a wave of peace wash over me. I felt myself melt

into the rock as I listened to the flowing stream rush by, the birds chirping around me, and the occasional call of a bullfrog. Directly in front of my field of vision was a twinkling orange light. I began to sing "Prophet" silently to myself several times. As I was singing "Prophet," I heard bells ringing. Soon after this, the sit exercise came to an end.

I went back up to the school for class. As time passed before I shared the experience with the group, I began to mentally talk myself out of the experience. I began to physically justify the light that I saw as spotlights mounted outside of the school that someone must have happened to turn on. Since this was my first spiritual class at the school, I thought that I was too new at this to experience the Divine Light of God. Boy was I wrong!

I felt multiple nudges from the inner Prophet that I should share my experience with the group. Since I was not sure if I had actually experienced something, I felt a good bit of hesitancy. After hearing many other individuals share their experiences during the exercise, I finally decided to share my experience with the group. When I shared, I received so much clarity on my experience. I learned that I was actually at the third Heaven during my experience. The calling card that I was at this Heaven was the color orange and the tinkling of bells. These colors and sounds that I thought I had made up or misconstrued from a physical light were actually God responding to me! By opening my heart and singing a love song to God, God responded by telling me that "I am loved by God." Had I not shared this experience with Del, I may have easily talked myself out of this Divine blessing, this gift of love from God. I may have missed that God not only heard me, but responded to me. The purpose of this exercise was to have the Prophet show us Divine Love. Sometimes this response from God may be so subtle that we are not even aware of it. Thank you Prophet for nudging me to share with the class, otherwise I may have totally missed this Divine gift of love from God!

Written by Michelle Kempf

9

The Golden Key

The Prophet gently unlocks our hearts and minds to his presence and to the Love of God at a pace that is perfect for each of us. To receive too much, too fast, would be counterproductive. The Prophet will often make his presence known with a blue light. This can happen in a dream or during the waking state. Either way, it is an invitation to accept the hand being offered and a reminder that we are never alone.

A few months after I attended my first spiritual retreat in 1998 at the Nature Awareness School I had a very special dream. At the retreat I learned that my dreams were real experiences worth paying attention to and that I could learn, grow, and have spiritual adventures in my dreams as Soul.

In my dream I was walking in a meadow along a crystal clear stream that seemed to sparkle as it meandered through the green grass. The sunlight seemed to illuminate everywhere I walked even though it was daytime. As I walked, I came to a blue flower next to the stream that became animated and seemed to want to show me something. The bright blue flower turned a bit and it seemed to be pointing to a rock near the stream with its little leaves. It sort of nodded and said, "hey - look over here." I looked at and around the rock but did not notice anything in particular but I had this feeling that there was something very special going on; I just had not recognized it yet. I looked back at the blue flower and it was pointing to the rock. I then turned the rock over and hidden beneath it was a golden key. The key had golden light shining all around it. Reaching down, I picked up the glowing key and held it in front of me with both my hands. Holding the key I felt light, free, and a warm love around me. I took the key on my journey and woke up feeling very light and happy.

When I was given this dream I was excited but didn't know what it meant at the time, but I knew it was very special. I did not know much about Prophets or the Heavenly worlds, but I had begun singing HU and had started to pay more attention to my dreams. Even though I did not recognize it at the time, this was a gift from God through His Prophet. God was reaching out to me in a way I could accept and understand without shocking my mind.

Early on the Prophet would let me be aware of his presence with a flash of blue light or in this case a blue flower and show me the way to something new. The blue light of the flower was showing me the way to a better life that is fulfilling the dreams of Soul. Because of my spiritual teacher Del Hall, over time, I have been taught to recognize and become fluent in the language and nature of the Divine. This has been accomplished by the personal experiences that have blessed my life since becoming a student at the Nature Awareness School. These experiences have given me a whole new life in which I feel very blessed to be living. The golden key I was given years ago has unlocked my heart to my true Divinity, God's endless Love, and the Heavenly worlds.

Written by Mark Snodgrass

10

God Rained Down His Light

I wonder how many people have witnessed the awesome Light or Sound of God, but have no reference for what they experienced? To accept and be grateful for the experience, one must first recognize its value. Having a living spiritual teacher who knows the "Language of the Divine" can truly help.

During graduate school I believe that I was led by God to live with Dorothy, an elderly lady on a farm in Delaware. On June 12, 1993 while reading a book about time being an illusion, all of a sudden my ears were full of the sound of the ocean. I shook my head to try to dislodge what I thought was water from swimming in the ocean the day before. But the loud sound of ocean waves continued for what seemed like a very long time. When the sound stopped I heard Chipper the dog barking.

I went to the back door to see what was going on with Dorothy's dog. As I peeked into her sitting room I saw Dorothy lying on the couch. I somehow knew I would need to perform CPR on her so I turned her from her side onto her back. When I turned her, her right eye opened and all this incredible light came pouring out of her eye. It was so beautiful. I also knew that I was witnessing something profound, and that what surrounded us was beyond this earthly world. I remember looking up toward the ceiling knowing that Dorothy, as Soul, was leaving. As this was happening the dog continued to bark. I believe the dog also knew that Dorothy was leaving us in the physical.

This experience stayed with me. It was not until two years later when I began attending classes at the Nature Awareness School that I learned what I had experienced and witnessed was the Light and Sound of God! There I've been blessed to experience the Light of God again and in many ways. During the second weeklong retreat I attended, I was sitting quietly in the woods and saw a bright white flash of light. It was as if someone had a huge camera flash bulb and took a photograph, but I knew otherwise. I also experienced, while lying down in my dark tent, points of light appearing as if the stars in the sky were on the ceiling above me. I have experienced the blue Light of God in my spiritual eye, which represents to me the presence of my spiritual guide.

Divine Spirit gently allowed me to see these gifts of the Light of God, all the while caressing, comforting, and strengthening me to accept more of God's Love. The blue Light of God began to appear in my spiritual eye when my physical eyes were closed. This happened most when I sang HU. Sometimes God would make His Presence known to me and I could feel His Love and peace.

Now I attend retreats at the Nature Awareness School several times a year. During a recent class Del, the Prophet, led the group in a HU sing. As I sat with my eyes closed singing this love song to God, I heard the sound of rushing wind and then I heard rainfall. Outside it was physically calm with a clear and dry sky. Spiritually I saw all of us standing together and being showered upon with huge raindrops of light. This real spiritual experience was a profound gift and beyond beautiful! I was privileged to witness these Souls being graced with God's abundant Love. Everyone in the group received the Divine gift with an openness of faith, love, trust, and humility.

Written by Moira Cervone

11

Wild Edible and Golden Light

One of the most popular and fun outdoor skills courses we used to offer was the "Wild Edible Plant Weekend." Folks really loved the transformation from looking out at a sea of green to actually seeing individual plants and learning how to identify and use them. It is amazing how many things are right before our eyes that we do not see until someone shows us how to truly look.

About eighteen years ago I attended a "Wild Edible Plant Weekend" at the Nature Awareness School. It was my second class on the mountain. During the weekend class Del took us on a walk to identify some of the specific plants we were learning about in class. The group of us came to a patch of Plantain. Del was describing how much he loved this plant and how many uses it had medicinally. You could just feel the love he had for this little plant in his voice as he spoke about its benefits. He then picked a few leaves to show us some of the details. The leaves were a shinny dark green with parallel veins found on the under side. As he was holding them in his hands I began to see a golden glow of light start at his hands and ascend up to his arms! I watched in awe! I wondered if I was seeing things — I blinked and rubbed my eyes. Nothing had changed except the golden light began to glow brighter and brighter! I looked around and noticed that no one else was seeing what I was singularly honored to see.

I filed this experience away but did not forget how it had touched my heart. I continued to process, on my own, what the experience really meant. I knew what I saw was real and that it had really happened. This was at a time in my life that I was hungry to learn more about the Divine and the Love of God. I had read in scripture that God has love for all of us and for all living things.

The next class I attended I spoke to Del of my experience with the golden light. He very simply said maybe it was God's Love coming through him. Since I was the only one that saw the golden light I felt very grateful to have such a personal gift. I believe the gift was personal because I have always had a special love of plants, flowers, and trees. It was years later that I also learned more about Del's spiritual connection with the Divine as a Prophet of God and the real reason I was so blessed that day. This was my first understanding many years ago of the Love of God being expressed in golden light.

Written by Nancy Nelson

12

The Prophet Shows His True Self

There are times when the curtain of "reality" is pulled back and we are allowed to see things as they truly are. We will never be shown more truth than we can handle at any given moment. So trust in God's perfect timing that you will "see" when the time is right, and remember - there is always more.

During one of my first classes at the Nature Awareness School I was blessed to see the light and love of the Prophet. I was listening to him as he was speaking with another student and he began to turn into light. His arms and legs began to glow, and then his torso began to change. I watched in amazement as his whole body turned into a ball of light. I was seeing the Prophet as Soul, as his true self. He then turned to face me; I could feel so much love coming through the light that he was sending to me. I began to look around the room and noticed that no one else seemed to be reacting to this. Everyone was looking directly at the Prophet but no one was seeing what I was seeing. This was a gift especially for me.

I turned to my girlfriend, who is now my wife, and she was also showing no reaction to what was happening. I leaned over, whispering, and asked if he did this all the time. She just smiled at me with a knowing look in her eye. The Prophet stayed in his Soul body until just before the end of the session. That is when he came back to his physical body.

After this I learned that the Prophet can teach students in many ways. He can teach each one of us individually while at the same time teaching the group as a whole. However he teaches, we all receive the lessons that are right for us. I am so grateful to the Prophet for sharing his light and love with me.

Written by Anthony Allred

13

The Light and Sound of God

There are beautiful examples in holy books of people experiencing the Light and Sound of God. Many can accept the truth in this, yet some have a hard time accepting that it still happens in this day and age. I can assure you that it does. God can shower His Light and Love on anyone, anytime. This in no way takes away from the service of those from the past. Instead, it glorifies and testifies to the continuing magnitude of a loving God who knows each and every one of us.

Many have heard of or read about the Light of God – God's Light. There are references of the Light of God in The Bible. One example is Jesus saying, "I am the light of the world" (John 8:12). Another example is about Saint Paul, then Saul, while traveling on the road to Damascus saw a light from Heaven, brighter than the sun, blazing around him and his companions (Acts 26:13).

My first experience with the Light of God was during one of my first classes as a student at the Nature Awareness School, almost fifteen years ago. My teacher, a Prophet of God, was leading the class of many students in a guided contemplation. Together we sang HU, a love song to God. I could feel God's Love and Presence all around me. In the darkness of the unlit room, I began seeing beautiful swirling colors of blue light in front of me. I could see this beautiful blue light with my eyes open and with them closed. Then a blue light in the shape of a heart appeared before me. I felt God's Love with me and within me, Soul.

The next day Del gave the class the opportunity to share experiences from the guided contemplation. I shared my experience of the blue light and the blue heart. Del explained that the blue light and blue heart are a calling card of the Prophet who was letting me know that he loves me and is always with me. My heart filled with love, joy, and deep appreciation for this gift of love from God! Throughout the years as a student at the school, I have been blessed with numerous experiences and blessings with the Light of God. Sometimes the light is blue, sometimes golden, and sometimes a brilliant white light.

I have also been blessed with the gift from the Divine of learning about the Sound of God – God's Voice. I am so blessed to have had many experiences with the Sound of God. The Sound or Voice of God is in everything, as is the Light of God. Everything and everyone – every Soul – is made of the Light and Sound of God. It is the Divine Spirit of God. It is also known as the Holy Ghost or the Holy Spirit, and other names. It is the life force from God, which can be seen and heard with our spiritual eyes and ears, and even with our physical eyes and ears, when we have the awareness to see and hear them. In the Bible there are references of the Sound of God. One is at Pentecost when the Apostles were all together in one place and "suddenly a sound like a blowing of a violent wind came from Heaven . . . all of them were filled with the Holy Spirit" (Acts 2:2).

I am blessed to have heard the Sound, the Voice of God in many forms, with both my spiritual and physical ears. Often when singing HU at a class at the school, or at home, I hear the Sound of God as music. Music "not of this world." Music of the Spheres. It is a music unlike any type or genre of music of this Earth, a sound impossible to reproduce with any musical instrument or singer's voice, and difficult if not impossible to describe or explain in words. It is a sound that I hear only while I am singing HU. As a musician, I know that hearing this special music is a very personal gift of God's Love to me.

While singing HU sometimes I hear the Voice of God as sounds of low, warm, soothing tones. While I cannot hear or decipher actual words, when I hear it I am filled with love, peace, joy, and comfort – all beautiful gifts of God's Love.

I am so very appreciative of and grateful to the Prophet for these amazing gifts of the Light and Sound of God, these gifts of love, and for the blessing of having the eyes and ears to see and hear them. I am so grateful for the HU.

Written by Cathy Sandman

14

Creator Please "Show Me Love"

*"Can you accept that you have seen the Light of God?"
was the question posed to the author of this piece.
What if this was your experience, could you accept a
blessing of this nature?*

It was dusk as I sat upon a small log beside the pond. Nightfall was gently rolling in upon this evening in the mountains. The setting was at a spiritual retreat at the Nature Awareness School about twenty years ago. My spiritual teacher Del had prepared our class to participate in a spiritual exercise called "Show Me Love." Each student found a "sit area" somewhere near the pond. It was a time to slow down the inner and outer pace for an opportunity to invite Divine Spirit more consciously into our hearts. This was a new experience for me back then. We were asked to approach this spiritual exercise with the attitude of not expecting anything, yet being open and receptive to whatever Divine Spirit may want to show us. To help us relax it was suggested to look at the landscape using wide-angle vision. It is a technique that uses all of your senses to help one become more aware of your surroundings. Sitting quite still I could see the sand beach, the pond, willows, birds, bats catching insects, a small patch of buttercup flowers, and dusk becoming nightfall. Bullfrogs sang and there was a soft breeze. Now relaxed I began to sing HU. Del taught us the HU song, an ancient name for God. It is the most pure prayer known. It is sung without expecting anything in return from the Creator. It is simply a way to say I love you. I sang HU for what seemed five to ten minutes. Then I prayed, Creator please "Show Me Love," sitting quietly with eyes closed learning to listen with my heart.

Very soon I began to smell the most fragrant scent of flowers. I had chosen the log to sit upon because of the buttercups that were beside it. As a child I admired the buttercup, yet knew it did not have such a large fragrance. I peeked at the buttercups, and then resumed the spiritual exercise. Next I began to hear people talking and walking past me in conversation. I thought they did not hear our teacher say to respect everyone's space during this time. We would have time after the exercise to share our experiences. I peeked to see who was talking and no one was anywhere near. Slightly confused I sat quietly with eyes closed and continued to pray, Creator please "Show Me Love." Once again I was disturbed by what seemed to be spotlights that were shining upon me. I opened my eyes and saw where the light was coming from. There appeared to be two huge round spotlights uphill from the pond beside Del and Lynne's home. They lit up the entire area with white light as though it was daytime. The lights seemed to be suspended in air as though on a wire moving gently up and down from a breeze. One was slightly larger than the other, appearing at least three feet wide. The light diffused around their circumferences. I was so puzzled by the lights being turned on and people talking during the spiritual exercise, that I opted to share only about the scent of flowers when we gathered afterwards to discuss our individual experiences. I did not want to insult others for what I thought at the time to be disruptions to the spiritual exercise.

Class was over for the evening and I had a strong nudge to walk up the hill to the house and find those spotlights. While searching the area Del arrived on silent feet and said, "Who's there?" I replied, "It's me, Ann. I'm looking for the spotlights that someone turned on during the show me love exercise." Del said quite clearly that they did not have any spotlights and asked, "Can you accept that you have seen the Light of God?" His words were a shocking contrast to my assumptions. His words left me speechless as he continued on into his home. My innate trust for Del allowed me to consider his question regarding my experiences. In time I was able to accept the realization and blessings received during the "Show Me Love" exercise that night. The Creator showed me spiritual light, spiritual sound, and spiritual scent! They were very clear ways of God showing me love. I needed time to grow into those realizations.

It is precious and necessary to have a spiritual teacher who understands the ways of Divine Spirit. Del taught me how to have and to understand my experience with the Light and Sound of God (the Holy Spirit). Then my world began to open up. I have grown to know that Divine Spirit communicates directly to all Souls. I am blessed to have been offered the spiritual tools to experience God's Love so directly. Knowing spiritual truths from experience has brought me a deep peace of heart. This peace is with me always.

When the Light of God visits in any form, be it lighting up the night or a tiny flash of light, it is a privilege to be conscious that Divine Spirit is communicating with me. Lighting up the night was in part a way to help me break through learned beliefs that the Light of God speaks only to those who wear religious robes or saints from the past. To grow in communication with Divine Spirit, heart to heart, is the great blessing of life.

Written by Ann Atwell

15

God's Light Gives Peace to a Troubled Heart

Experiencing the Light of God can provide healing and comfort. Sadness, guilt, regrets, worry, and so on, can be washed away in Its presence. When bathed in the Light it also helps us to see clearly, including seeing ourselves and the actions that are holding us back. This combination of God's Love, truth, and action on our part, can lift us out of the darkest hole.

Back in 2001, I was going through a difficult time. I was facing a lot of change all at once and was feeling overwhelmed with sadness and a bit of fear for my future. I was twenty-eight years old and had recently bought my first home with my partner of eight years. I worked from home at this time. A few months before we bought our house together I had gotten in some legal trouble. I was waiting for my court date to find out whether I could keep my driver's license or not. This was causing me stress.

About eight months after we had bought our home, my partner and I broke up. This was largely due to my shortcomings, although in hindsight it was the best thing for both of us. We had gradually been growing apart but bought a home in the hopes that it would make our relationship stronger. It didn't. Shortly after we broke up I lost my driver's license for six months. In a very short period of time I went from a new home where I had my office, to no home, and no place to work, and no driver's license. Not to mention the split with my partner. It was a difficult time in my life.

I moved out of the house into my younger brother's home and rented a room there. This was humbling to say the least, yet I needed this lesson. I always knew that God was with me through this. Still I was sad and guilt ridden for my sense of failure. I had no spiritual tools but prayer, and it turns out, that is all I needed to get me through this time. I was not in any formal religion nor was I particularly "Godly." However, I found out that even the "least of thy servants" can be comforted and shown God's Grace during times of need.

I was sleepless for the third night in a row, and as I laid in my rented room and bed crying - I prayed to God. I prayed for comfort and to be able to rest. Just then, I felt a warm blanket of blue light come over me. The light was in my inner vision and it was very loving and peaceful. I fell asleep looking at this light and I woke up refreshed. The feeling of sadness and regret was replaced with hope and renewal. I took responsibility for my mistakes and took steps to rectify them.

I changed the way that I lived my life and soon after I found a spiritual path that was right for me. I really think that this time of change, even though difficult, was the turning point in my life for the better. It showed me that God cared about me enough to comfort me and now I wanted to do my part too.

Written by Tash Canine

16

Light and Love at Vision Rock

Experiencing spiritual light is one of the most direct ways to connect with God and feel God's Love. The Light of God comes in many forms and may be experienced in a dream or during the waking state. Either way, it is a profound blessing and one that still happens in this day and age.

How do I describe an experience that I had not consciously known in this lifetime, and that really has no words? I came to the Nature Awareness School for a Nature Awareness Weekend class but it was so much more than a weekend of learning nature skills. One of the activities we did that weekend was to take a nature hike that brought us to Vision Rock. Vision Rock is a rock ledge overlook with an incredible view. We were invited to go out on the rock, sit quietly, relax, and experience some quiet time.

The day was overcast and cloudy so there really was not much of a view.

I closed my eyes and was saying a quiet prayer of gratitude when my inner vision was filled with light. This surprised me because I did not know what to make of it. I opened my eyes to see if the sun had come out but it had not and when I closed my eyes the inner light was still shining. I opened and closed my eyes a few more times and had the same experience. Not only was I experiencing God's Light in my inner vision, but it was also touching my heart. I can not give specifics on what happened but something was opened and touched and I was changed. A river of tears came out. The Light of God had touched my Divine self – Soul. Soul recognized this sacred moment and was responding.

After attending the Nature Awareness School for a while I came to realize this was the Light of God I had experienced, and have continued to experience because of the teachings I have received. I have been graced with so many beautiful and amazing experiences since the Light and Love of God touched me twenty years ago. My life was changed and continues to change with greater peace, joy, and love in my heart and life. God and His Light and Love are still very active today. Beautiful and life changing experiences like those that are written in the Bible are still actively going on today to ordinary people. I am so grateful that I am blessed to have a teacher that can guide me on the inner and outer to recognize the blessings of God.

Written by Renee Walker

17

Waking up to the Light of God

The following is another incredible example of seeing, and feeling connected to, the Light of God. Countless students through the years have experienced this blessing in various forms. This is something we do not take for granted, but continue to be deeply grateful.

I have always felt a strong connection to Divine Spirit. All my life I remember reading stories of people who had these marvelous experiences with Spirit. I read about those experiences in the Bible, in the histories of some Saints, and in some of the songs we would sing in church when I was growing up. I always knew in my heart that a very deep and profound relationship with Divine Spirit was "out there somewhere."

In one of the early wilderness survival classes I took at the Nature Awareness School, we were building "debris huts" in which we would sleep the rest of the week. A debris hut is a shelter made of sticks laid across a long pole. Piled on top of this framework are layers and layers of leaves to provide insulation against the cold. Leaves are also stuffed inside as a kind of sleeping bag. The hut is built small, so there is not much empty space for your body heat to warm up.

The first night that I slept in the hut, I was awakened by an extremely bright light shining in my face. I thought it was someone shining a flashlight right at me. I sat bolt upright and just looked at that light. It wasn't only a light though. With the light there was a connection to something else. I felt a presence connected to it. I looked at this very intently for a while, and after a few minutes I lay back down and went back to sleep.

The next morning I remembered this very vivid experience. When I shared it in class the next day, and described the "flashlight," Del just smiled, nodded and said "hmm, flashlight" in a very knowing way.

Del's reaction made me re-think this experience. I started looking at this from a deeper perspective. There was much more to this experience than just a "flashlight" in my face waking me up. Suddenly it occurred to me that the roof of the debris hut was only six inches above my nose. As real as it felt, there was no possible way I could have sat up and looked at this light in my physical body. I would have knocked myself out against a tree branch sitting up so quickly. I know now that the light was the Light of God. The presence I felt was Divine Spirit. It wasn't just a random light, like a ship passing in the night. It was right there in my face, a direct personal experience with Divine Spirit. God was reaching out to me and interacting with me in a very profound and very personal way. I was being "woken up" in the spiritual sense.

Since that time, twenty years ago, I have had many more personal experiences with the Divine and the Light of God. Each experience is unique and just as precious as the first one I recounted here.

Written by Paul Nelson

18

My Personal Invitation

*One of the very first things shared with new seekers is
the importance of gratitude. It is something that one
never outgrows the need for. The beauty of gratitude is
that it opens your heart to the many blessings of God.
One of the greatest blessings being the Prophet, which
God always has on Earth to help show His children the
way home. Those with the eyes to see will recognize this
eternal teacher within its current physical incarnation.*

In 1996, as a result of a brochure we received,
my wife and I decided to take a class at the
Nature Awareness School. Neither one of us
really knew where the brochure came from or
how we got it, but it appeared at the perfect
time and changed our lives forever. During one
of my first classes I was offered the opportunity
of a lifetime, though at the time I did not
understand my good fortune. Since then,
through an incredible spiritual journey and
adventure, I have learned about my true self and

have developed a more personal relationship with God.

God, through his Prophet Del Hall, opened my eyes to see more clearly what is truly real and valuable in life, and offered me the way back to my true home in the Heart of God. I did not understand what I was being offered at that time, but something deep inside of me recognized something extraordinary in what I heard in Del's voice and saw in his eyes. One afternoon we did a spiritual exercise using a technique called wide-angle vision. During the exercise my spiritual eyes seemed to open more fully. I knew I had been given a gift. I could now clearly perceive things differently, with a new view, and a deeper awareness. Everything looked, felt, and sounded different. I experienced a depth and richness in a way I had not before.

Later in the day my wife and I wanted to talk with Del. I remember noticing something unusual about this conversation. In the middle of the busy classroom everything appeared to move around us as if we were not in the same physical space as the other students present. It was as if we were in some kind of special quiet protected bubble. Near the end of the conversation Del mentioned that before we went to sleep we should think of some things that we were grateful for in our lives. He said gratitude would open our hearts to Divine Love, which we had just been talking about. Then he asked us to pay attention to our dreams and to fill him in the next morning.

Before I went to sleep I did as he suggested and thought of the things, people, and experiences that I am grateful for in my life. Shortly after, in that in-between state where you are not fully awake and have not yet drifted off to sleep, I saw a bright orange and yellow light dance into my view. This light looked like a ball of fire or like the burning bush Moses saw that is referred to in the Bible. I had never experienced anything like this light before. The ball of spiritual light, looking like fire, changed into an intense white light, which slowly turned into what I could best describe as a blue tinted moon or ball of blue light. This ball of light rose up and out of a beautiful shimmering body of water and then Del spiritually appeared before me. He gestured to join him and then we walked off together. In the morning, before I could share anything about my experience from the night before, Del casually mentioned that in the dream state he had come and taken my wife and I to a spiritual temple to meet "his Boss." How could he have known what we had experienced last night? Both my wife and I remembered going somewhere with him in our dreams, but not anything after going or any of the specifics.

It has taken many years for me to gain an understanding and to recognize the depth of the blessings that were offered during that early weekend retreat. I did not have the awareness or conditioning at that time to remember details of where Del took us on the inner planes. But over time with his loving guidance, more experiences, training, practice, and grace, I have been able to remember and benefit more and more from these travels into the inner worlds. Through these experiences and Del's guidance I have learned how much God really loves us and always has one of His Prophets to guide us Home to Him. I wish everyone could know how much God loves them.

Since that early class I have been escorted by the Prophet to many of God's spiritual Temples of learning. As Soul, a child of God, I can be taken by God's chosen representative to learn more about who I truly am and why I am here. It is through the guidance of the Prophet who shares experience with God's Light, Sound, and especially God's Love that we come to know and learn more about God. In hindsight, I realize that on that night many years ago, through Del, that God had personally extended His hand and love to me, and I accepted. My relationship with the Prophet of God has made it possible for me to truly accept God's Love and Grace.

Del is now offering others a similar opportunity to the one he offered me many years ago. A chance to consciously go home to Heaven, to visit God, and experience the love He has for you. I am so very grateful I accepted!

Written by Jason Levinson

.

19

Blue Light Brought Peace

We are not alone. God loves us and always has a living Prophet here on Earth to help, teach, protect, and comfort us. Ultimately - to lead us home to God. This Divine Guide can appear to you as a blue light in your inner vision or in the physical itself. Either way, it is joyous proof of being loved and not alone.

When I first moved away from home it was a very stressful time. I was in a totally new area and everything was unfamiliar. The stresses of moving, plus my first college classes, were taking a toll. I was having a hard time finding a new balance so I prayed for help.

One night I was sitting in my dorm room working on homework. Out of the corner of my eye, I saw a brilliant flash of blue light. It was accompanied by a profound sense of peace. From the spiritual teachings I had received at the Nature Awareness School, I knew that this was no ordinary light, it was the Light of God;

referred to in so many spiritual scriptures. The Light of God is one of the special ways, which God communicates to us. The blue light in particular indicated the presence of a high level spiritual guide. His presence also brought the profound sense of peace, the peace that I had been so hungry for and had prayed for.

Twenty-four hours later, I stepped foot on the property of the Nature Awareness School for another weekend retreat. I know the Prophet used the blue light to prepare me to get the most out of the weekend. This retreat was the beginning of a whole new leg of not only my spiritual journey, but my life! It brought joy and balance back into my life. Now I know that a spiritual guide is always with me, an ever-present source of comfort, guidance, protection, and inspiration.

Written by David Hughes

20

Sweet Dreams

Singing HU and asking for a dream before falling asleep helps you tune in and raise up to receive and better remember the experience. Most importantly it is also a form of drawing nigh. Anyone seeking a closer relationship with the Divine should consider this sacred principle. When you draw nigh to God, God will respond.

"Sweet Dreams" with a smiley face was written on the white board by Del, my spiritual teacher at the Nature Awareness School in Love, Virginia. It was one of the first classes I had attended back in the 1990's. When I arrived that day I looked at the grassy dam that held back the waters from the pond and was excited to place my one-person backpacking tent as close to the water as possible.

As I crawled into my tent and made efforts to get comfortable in my sleeping bag I listened to the night sounds of bullfrogs, birds, and insects. The air seemed alive with sound. I was very excited and asked Divine Spirit to please bring me a dream that was in my best spiritual interest and help me remember the dream. Del had made those suggestions during class with the option to share our dream experiences in class the next morning.

I sang HU, a pure prayer to God. In a moment I was aware of three spiritual beings kneeling on either side of me. They were made of white translucent light. Silently they wrapped me in what felt like a very soft, deep, downy comforter. The thin sleeping mat on which I was resting seemed to disappear. I was wrapped in this comforter as a child may be swaddled in a blanket of love by its father or mother. I felt the gentlest peace and love fill my being and was aware of being lifted up. The next morning I woke in the physical and felt well rested, refreshed, and happy with the memory of the amazing experience of being tucked in at bedtime as never before.

It seems remembering those moments when Soul was raised up in consciousness was more important than remembering the dreams that continued on through the night. The experience helped me grow in realization that I am Soul, a Divine spark of God. As Soul I can travel safely under the guidance of my spiritual teacher. I have learned that I am loved and given the experiences that are perfect for my spiritual unfoldment. God's timing is perfect.

Over time and daily practice of singing HU, I have come to know that the spiritual beings who nourished me with comfort and love are the Prophet and his co-workers. That experience showed me I am Divinely guided and protected when traveling the vast inner worlds in the dream state. It is very reassuring to be in the presence of the one who knows the way, knows me, and knows my needs on my journey home to the Heart of God. Once you are touched by the Hand of God, it is not easily forgotten. The experience of God's Love is different from the experience of human love and cannot be measured or explained in words. The human standard of what I thought love to be has changed as my view of Divine Love grows through personal experiences with the Divine. With a sincere intent and prayer in your heart to experience Divine Love, it can happen. I am grateful for the outer and inner guidance available through the Prophet, the Comforter of our time.

Written by Ann Atwell

21

A Sound of God

*The Light and Sound of God are the twin aspects of the
Voice of, or the Word of God. Also known as the Holy
Ghost, Divine Spirit, and countless other names. Most
of the world is familiar with the idea of spiritual light.
Spiritual sound is less well known. It is however just as
important, if not more to the journey of Soul. The Light
of God illuminates the path, but ultimately it is the
sound we follow home to God.*

Twenty years ago during my first class at the
school, Del talked about how some students
were starting to hear the spiritual sound of flute
music. That one could actually hear spiritual
sound, a sound beyond what one could hear
with one's physical ears, was amazing to me and
beyond my frame of reference at the time. I had
never heard or read anything about spiritual
sound. I was blessed with an experience with the
Light of God that same week, but the other
aspect of the voice of the Divine, the Sound of

God, remained a mystery amid a sea of uncharted waters for me.

A year later, right after a spiritual retreat at the school, one that opened my heart to accepting more Divine Love, including the truth that we are all eternal Souls, I awoke in the middle of the night to the sound of the most beautiful flute music coming out of the Heavens. This beautiful Divine Sound spoke right to me, as Soul, and filled me with a joy and inner peace of a sort that I had never known before in this lifetime. It was truly God speaking to me, letting me know that I am loved.

Two years later when my heart was heavy from a relationship that had come to an end, and I was alone in nature trying to find some peace, I heard the flute music again. This time it went on for several days. I would not hear it every moment, but whenever I made the effort to listen, there it was, the most beautiful music of God, giving me peace in my heart and filling me with an unspeakable joy. I felt such gratitude for the classes at the Nature Awareness School that had opened me up spiritually so that I could hear the sound. I was far away from all family and friends but I was not alone, as I experienced the loving presence of the Voice of God through the beautiful sound. This presence has been with me from the beginning; only now I had the "ears" with which to hear it speak to me. The Nature Awareness School has been the most profound of blessings in my life, for the teachings within its classes are eternal ones that have provided me with the skills needed to tune into Divine Spirit and hear God's Voice.

Written by Roland Vonder Muhll

22

Welcome to the Temple

There is only a thin veil between our reality and the other spiritual realms. Whether we are aware of it or not we are all journeying to more fully understand this truth. There is no greater way to do this than to experience it for yourself. For twenty-five years my father, the Prophet, has been helping people to do just that. Below is but one example.

The fog was so thick I could barely see the pine tree next to the large rock I sat on. I was at my first weekend spiritual retreat at the Nature Awareness School during the final "sit exercise" of the class. We were all allowed to find a spot outdoors to sit, sing HU, and then ask the Divine a simple prayer to "show me love." There were many truths that Del, the Prophet, introduced in class that were so new and "out of the box" for me and that I was not yet ready to accept. Now, after nearly twenty years of countless experiences I have witnessed and personally experienced, his teachings are as self-evident to me as needing air to breathe or gravity, but back then they seemed alien and challenged my rigid yet fragile grasp of reality. The HU, that glorious love song to our Creator, was a spiritual tool that I immediately trusted on some deep level. It became and continues to be a steadying force through the calms and storms of life, and my compass, eternally pointing me to spiritual true north.

I sat on the rock that day, singing HU. I could not see any of the other students, though occasionally I could pick up the faint echoes of their HUs. Otherwise, I felt alone and secluded, much like I had my entire life. I awaited, unsure of what to expect next. I knew there was more, more out of this experience and more out of life, but felt clueless as to how to access whatever it was I was missing. I occasionally opened my eyes with my vision greeted only by the dense fog, which obscured nearly everything. Suddenly I was escorted out of my body and gently set down into what appeared to be a rotunda. I later came to know that I was at one of God's Temples, accessible not by physical travel, but by spiritual travel as Soul. I saw Del here in this inner temple in a garment of stunning white.

There were others there as well, dressed similarly. They descended the stairs each smiling like they knew and were expecting me. Showered with the Love of God, I was grateful they made me feel so welcome. Accompanying this Light was music equally Divine. It was angelic and Heavenly. It softly played, coaxing my heart open wider and wider. I could not pinpoint Its source. It seemed to come from everywhere at once. It reverberated in my heart, both soothing and energizing me. I felt as if I had died and gone to Heaven!

I was so stunned by what had just happened I opened my physical eyes. The dense fog still hung lazily in the air. Not only could I see hardly anything, but the contrast between fog and temple was startling. In the cool dull mist that enveloped the world I knew to be "real," I did not feel nearly as alive or real as I did in the temple. I opened and closed my eyes several more times. It was remarkable. I was not visualizing standing in the temple. I was not seeing it in my imagination or my mind's eye. I was really there! In fact, the inversion was so strong it felt like I was standing in this temple "imagining" I was sitting in the fog on a large rock!

When I returned from the sit exercise, I eyed the others in class closely. Had they experienced this too? Was this normal? No one was freaking out. As they shared their experiences I do not recall anyone mentioning visiting a Temple of God. Yet I could say, by the Grace of God, I had truly been. It is so amazing how God knows exactly what we need. Those early steps we take on the path of love, where our minds have finally relaxed and our hearts are opening, are precious. God might greet some Souls with deep peace, or soothing grace, or incredible gentleness. For me it was a warm welcome in a place of unsurpassed beauty and truth where I felt like I truly belonged. How grateful I am to be allowed entry into a Temple of God. That first conscious visit cemented for me several things. I am welcome in God's mansions, in His Temples. There is much, much more beyond what I see through the fog of life with my physical senses. And the simple spiritual tools that Del has shared with me have led to an incredible inner journey. More is out there and it is amazing!

I treasure this experience of nearly twenty years ago. Without it, how much love and life I might have missed! God loved me enough to give me the perfect experience for me that day. I was so full of questions and wanted to know more. It emboldened me to pursue a grand adventure of the heart and the courage to not discount what my heart knew to be true. Following my heart led to more classes and more experiences at the Nature Awareness School where many of my original questions – and beyond – have been answered. Maybe, like me, the sublime majesty of God's Heavens has you peeking to see if the fog is still there. Perhaps there is something that rings true to you like the HU does for me. Something faithful and rock solid to hold onto as you work your way through the fog of life and a step closer to your eternal home.

Written by Chris Comfort

Section Two

Section Two

Growing and Conditioning

After a new seeker has been blessed with their early experiences with God's Light, gradually they become more familiar with recognizing its presence. As they become spiritually strengthened they can more fully receive the blessings within the light. From this point on God's Light is an integral part of purifying the seeker and teaching God's ways and truth. The healing of their physical, emotional, mental, and spiritual selves can begin. Specific and useful information is bestowed upon Soul via God's Light and Sound. I can now teach both the mind and Soul simultaneously. It is a far more advanced approach to teaching the ways of God when the real eternal self, Soul, and the mind begin to work in unison, rather than battling one another.

Some of the testimonies in this section share how God's Light begins to remove mental passions that can block further spiritual growth.

Common barriers to real lasting growth are fear, vanity, extreme attachment to anything of this physical world, and feeling unworthy of God's Love. As the Prophet my presence and authorized use of God's Light can, over time, remove any blockages that exist between the individual, the Prophet, and God Himself! Experiences shared in this section continue to teach, acclimate, condition, and strengthen the seeker. Once a student is ready, I can safely guide them into the many Heavens for further instruction. Here they receive personal instruction to be determined by the Holy Spirit. This is the most perfect way to be taught, by the Voice of God, making your syllabus precise and personal.

Some individuals are even blessed to be taken all the way home to the Abode of God! As I help a student to grow, they begin to accept Divine Love and Divine Guidance daily. They now live a life of abundance! This abundance comes from recognizing, understanding, and living daily in God's Love and His ways. From a higher view in life one makes better decisions, has more love and gratitude, better priorities, more peace and joy. As the sacred relationship between the individual and myself grows in love and trust, I can more fully assist them in accomplishing their personal spiritual goals.

23

An Invitation From the Prophet

Singing HU is one of the purest ways for Soul to express its love to God. It is sung in loving gratitude with no thought of reward. However, being of a giving nature, many times God sends love right back to us. This love comes in many forms; peace, joy, an insight, a lifting of sadness, healing, clarity, spiritual light or sound, an invitation for a closer relationship with His Prophet, and on and on. Each Soul is known and loved personally and thus receives exactly what they need at that moment in their journey. What a joy to know we are heard.

Yesterday morning, a cool breeze caressed the late summer leaves as my children and I walked through the sunshine at the Nature Awareness School. With gratitude and joy we settled ourselves in for a HU Sing, an opportunity for those who love God to sing this ancient song of love to God as a group. Del Hall, my teacher and friend for more than twenty years, joyfully welcomed the group as he took his seat on the low, hand-made stage at the front the room.

Singing HU, an ancient name for God, is one of my daily joys; yet it is even more wonderful when done with a large group of Souls who love God. As Del, the Prophet of God began to sing, all of us quickly joined in a great harmony. With my eyes closed while I sang, I soon became aware of gentle waves of blue light rolling in. They seemed to come from where Del was sitting in front of the group and radiated out in all directions. I also became aware of another light, a beam of white light, which came straight down to Del, and then split into smaller beams which went outwards to each person in the group. As we gave love to God, so it was that God was giving love right back to us, but in greater measure! Still we continued to sing, and I felt that the rolling waves of blue light were growing stronger. They seemed to bounce off some distant shore and come back to us from behind. With each returning wave of light it seemed that each of us was being gently nudged towards the center, towards the Prophet, and towards that great beam of white light. By singing HU with the Prophet we were drawing nigh to God by our own free will, and in so doing, God was drawing nigh to us with this great embrace of light and love. I no longer saw the separate beams of white light going to each Soul, but rather saw that we were all joyfully within this great beam of God's Light and Love.

At some point our song came to an end and I felt a great peace and sense of completeness. With my physical eyes closed, I perceived a strong, but gentle blue light before me. This deep, rich, blue light edged with gold gently grew in size until it occupied most of my view. I knew in my heart that this beautiful blue light was an invitation from the Prophet, inviting those Souls present to come with him on a journey of discovery to find a closer relationship with the Creator, a deeper knowledge of one's own heart, and a greater acceptance of one's own Divinity. Having been on this greatest of all journeys for quite some time, I joyfully accepted the invitation knowing that there is always more, and the Prophet knows the way. On the inner I reached into the light and saw that I was already holding hands with the Prophet. The light grew in intensity and my heart filled even more with a deep peace beyond words. And then I wondered if some there were having their first conscious glimpse of Divine Light. With gratitude I remembered the first few times I had been blessed in that way. From experience, I knew that each person in the group would receive exactly the experience they needed. After a while, the light faded from my view; some insights gently arrived to answer questions and prayers in my heart. Still, the deep peace remained. God wants to share this peace and light with you as well. Will you accept the invitation?

Written by Timothy Donley

24

Bathed by God's Golden Light and Love

It is the Love of God that creates, sustains, and nurtures us. It is the food for Soul. One of the most direct ways to experience the Love of God is spiritual light. Within it nothing is lacking.

During a recent class at the Nature Awareness School I was blessed to experience God's Love in the form of golden light. We were singing HU, a love song to God, and as I was singing I became aware of a shower of golden love permeate the room. It was a soft golden white light that gently caressed and nurtured me. Light poured into the room, even though outside it was nighttime.

With the light came love and a sense of peace that only communion with the Divine can bring. Worries that I had brought with me and ones that I was not even aware of slowly washed away.

In that moment of experiencing God's Light, I needed nothing. I was completely content. It was a blessing to see the Love of God that showers upon us, but we do not always have the eyes to see. In this seemingly simple spiritual exercise of sending love to God by singing HU, I was blessed a thousand fold with peace and contentment. As you sow, so shall you reap. The love that I gave came back to me in abundance. What a gift!

Written by Molly Comfort

25

Love Thyself

*You are here on Earth to become more refined in your
ability to give and receive love. Of the two, more seem
to struggle with receiving, especially when it is from our
self. Regardless of how you "feel," the fact remains -
you are worthy.*

When I first came to the Nature Awareness
School I was shy and self-conscious, full of
anxiety and guilt, carrying a sadness around with
me as my own. I felt unworthy of God's Love
based on a false mental view of myself. It took
many experiences to break through this, to
realize I was looking at myself from my mind,
instead of viewing myself as Soul, my spiritual
side, my true self. Slowly, I quit beating myself
up as much, and began accepting that I am
worthy of God's Love. I am not the mistakes I
blew all out of proportion. I learned to forgive
and love myself.

An inner experience during a spiritual exercise at the Nature Awareness School helped me to see this truth more clearly. Del, the Prophet, took me on a journey to a Temple of God. It was beautiful beyond description and filled with God's Love. In the center, a beam of light was shining on an open book on a pedestal; God's Book. The Prophet encouraged me to read from it. I stepped into the beam and read "Love Thyself with all Thy Heart and Soul."

I knew I could no longer beat myself up or judge myself so harshly. I also realized that I could not truly love God until I could love Its creation, me, Soul, a particle of Its Holy Spirit. This helped me accept a profound Truth, "Soul exists because God loves it." My existence, every breath, every moment of life, is a gift from God to be cherished.

I am grateful to the Prophet for being with me every step of the way on my journey of growth and discovery, for his guidance, protection and truth. It is by accepting his hand, and the relationship that followed, that has allowed me to move from a limited and miserable view of myself to the boundless one of Soul. Surrendering my old ways of thinking, many based on half-truths and falsehoods, gives me the freedom to pursue a life of abundance.

Written by Gary Caudle

26

My Daughter Born By Spirit

Many times we are overly attached to a particular outcome or way of doing something without even knowing it. The more attached we are the more we tie God's hands in delivering His blessings. When we truly let go the situation can be born anew.

I am blessed to be the mom of three amazing, and beautiful girls. Eleven years ago, this journey of motherhood began. I loved being pregnant with my first child. Excitement, anticipation, worry, and joy all coexisting while we awaited her arrival. Being holistically minded, it was my deep desire to have a natural childbirth. My loving husband and I prepared as much as we possibly could, reading a plethora of books, and taking every birthing class offered in our area.

The big day was finally approaching. On June 7th, at 2:15 PM my water broke, and with it some complications arose. I was admitted to the hospital before labor truly began. A natural birth was still on the table, but as time ticked on, the outlook was looking less likely. I relied on the HU, one of my best spiritual tools to keep me calm. I felt peace and knew all would be fine. Five hundred miles away my sister-in-law was also waiting with anticipation. She kept checking in to see how labor was progressing. We went through the entire next day, and still no baby.

Exhausted at this point I gave in and they administered drugs to speed up labor. I finally yielded and accepted an epidural for the intense pain that labor brings on. On the evening of June 8th true labor was finally setting in. My sister-in-law went to bed that evening with us in her thoughts. She had a dream, and in that dream she saw a brilliant blue light gently push the baby from my womb. Meanwhile back at the hospital, at the exact same moment, I looked at my husband and said, "I need help, I need help, and I truly surrender!"

I felt a sudden and noticeable warmth in my womb and instantly had a rush of stamina. On June 9th at 2:15 AM, exactly thirty-six hours to the minute of my water breaking, we gazed eyes upon our sweet baby girl. It was the Light of God that touched my baby and helped her come into this world. Even though earlier in the day I sang HU, and I felt peace, I still had an attachment to the way I wanted things to work out. I was not even aware of my attachments until I verbally surrendered the outcome. My sister-in-law's dream confirmed what I was feeling in those same moments. In my hour of need God heard my cry and gave me one of the greatest joys of my life; my daughter.

Written by Kate Hall

27

A Golden Lifeline of Love

*We are living on Earth during unprecedented times.
The opportunity for spiritual growth in this lifetime is
almost unlimited. God is directly seeking a more
personal relationship with each and every one of us.
The Hand of the Divine is stretched out - will you
accept it?*

I was at a spiritual retreat at the Nature
Awareness School. Del was guiding us in a
spiritual exercise that helped us tune out
distractions of the outer world and go on the
inner to seek guidance, counsel, and wisdom
from the Holy Spirit.

We opened our hearts to Divine Love by
thinking of things in our lives that we were truly
grateful for and then we sang HU, a beautiful
love song to God. I felt totally safe and was
receptive to whatever experiences and
adventures might come. I could see violet and
blue lights swirling in my inner vision. My eyes

were closed so I knew the light was not physical in nature. This was spiritual light.

This inner vision became very bright. There was a beam of white light that came into view and out of this came "golden threads." One of these golden threads was being offered to each of us. It was a gift of love direct from God. We were told that if we wanted we could choose to accept it. I did. I reached out, took hold of it, and tied it under my arms like a harness. I wanted to make the most of this opportunity and I wanted this connection to stay secure. I knew that what was being offered was priceless beyond my understanding, and I never wanted to let go of It, or It let go of me. If I ever encountered difficult times or got lost in the passing parade – the non-eternal distractions of the material world; this golden cord could be a lifeline and help me find my way back home.

Even though I have not always been conscious of it being there, I know this has been a spiritual lifeline for me and has blessed me in so many ways. It is a connection between my heart and God's Heart. The love that flows through it goes both ways. In looking back I see it was an offer to have a personal relationship with God. This relationship has grown into a true love. This love connection nourishes and sustains me every day. It has brought comfort, peace, and clarity during challenging times and has helped me learn and grow from those lessons of living. It makes "ordinary days" extra-ordinarily satisfying and full of joy, wonder, and richness. I treasure this experience and so appreciate this precious gift of God's Grace and enduring Love.

Written by Lorraine Fortier

28

Broken Neck Healed by the Light

In this story of protection and being healed by God's Light there is much to be grateful about. It shows there is no limit to what God can do, including healing someone before the injury even occurs.

Last summer I was in a car accident. The accident itself was a miracle because no one was seriously injured. I was run off the highway, crossed the median, and stopped right before oncoming traffic. The other car was pushed back into our traffic lanes but was not hit by other cars. I drove home that evening and went to get an x-ray the next day just to make sure I was not injured. The doctor came in and told me "don't move," a C-collar was placed on my neck and I was laid down. I thought it must be some kind of joke as I had been walking around all night. The doctor said that the x-ray showed a fractured C6 vertebra, a broken neck. She showed my husband the x-ray and he could visibly see where my bone was misplaced. I was transferred to the ER, and as I lay there for a few hours, I was praying to God, as were my family and friends. Doctors were discussing a possible surgery for that evening. I had a CT scan to get a better image and the doctor said "It must have been a bad x-ray; you don't have a fractured neck." My husband and I looked at each other and knew, it was not a bad x-ray, it was a healing. My husband had seen the x-ray with his own eyes.

Not long after this I was attending a HU Sing at the Nature Awareness School when the Prophet, my spiritual guide, took me back to an experience on the inner that I had earlier in the year (before my accident). During this experience, I was touched by God's Light! I was bowed in reverence as God's Light shone down on the back of my neck. To be touched by the Light of God was an amazing life changing experience! I know God loves me! I felt so much love, joy, warmth, peace, and strength during this experience that I was not paying attention to where I was touched. I was focused on the immense blessing it was that I was actually being touched by God's Light. It was not until I was shown this experience again that I realized I was specifically touched right at my C6 vertebra. I was immediately taken back to the accident and saw a direct connection between these two experiences. I know the Light of God touching my neck that day was a healing. Wow!

I am so very grateful and appreciative for the Love of God and I am blessed to see God's Love throughout my daily life.

Written by Emily Allred

29

Healing Pink and Orange Light

When you are blessed to know God's Love it builds the trust needed to get through life's challenges. To be confident, that even though sometimes very painful, our experiences are helping us to grow in our ability to give and receive love. The greater the challenge, the greater the opportunity - even though it might take years to accept and understand the blessings of growth. Our trials are not punishment from God - they are opportunities to grow closer. In the following story the author prays for a dear friend going through a very sad time and is witness to God's healing Light in response.

I have been blessed with an amazing best friend since childhood. When we were in elementary school we spent every possible waking moment together. In middle school she moved about thirty minutes away and we begged our willing mothers to drive us back and forth. Then in high school I moved several states away and during college we found ourselves on opposite ends of the country. The periods of time between visits and distance between us might have been extended but it had no diminishing effect on our friendship. Six months could pass without talking and then with one phone call it was like there had been no separation at all. Now as adults the physical distance between us has become only a few states and we are able to see each other one or two times per year.

She has been there for me through many of my significant moments; losing my mother at the age of sixteen, getting married, and being blessed with two children. I have been there for her through many of her significant moments; losing her beloved childhood dog, her marriage, and her journey to motherhood. Since we were kids we have both dreamed of becoming mothers. We talked about different names and how many kids we hoped to have one day.

She was blessed to conceive a baby girl in 2013 and was due to deliver in June of 2014. We celebrated in the usual ways and I shared stories of my pregnancy, sleepless days with a newborn, and how motherhood had brought about a deep love in me beyond my wildest imagination. She was on the doorstep of her dream becoming a reality. It never occurred to me that something heartbreaking would change the course of our lives. Tragically during her delivery she lost her baby and suffered severe physical trauma to her own body. Feelings of shock, helplessness, and disbelief hit me harder than I can recall ever feeling in this lifetime. I was hundreds of miles away when I heard the news and could not bear the feeling that I had zero power or ability to ease the pain for my dear friend and her family. I could not even imagine what she was experiencing.

I wept, prayed, and sang HU for twenty-four hours straight after hearing the news. I prayed with everything in me to God to please lift even one ounce of the pain and suffering from her heart. Slowly God showed me that I was not entirely powerless. With God anything is possible and I am so grateful to know that prayers are real and that they provide the sacred opportunity to express our feelings directly to God. I am so grateful that the Prophet has given me the tools to express my compassion and the deep trust to know that we are all in God's hands. I do not know mentally why her life took this course but I trust God that there was a reason that it did.

The first day after hearing the news my prayers were answered and I was blessed with a dream and a spiritual visit to my friend. In the dream her baby was alive and healthy and being cared for and nurtured by two loving Souls in Heaven. I was able to hold her and feel the warmth of her soft skin. It brought me peace to know that her daughter was being watched over and hope that maybe one day this Soul could try again to become her child. The mother and child love bond they share transcends their physical separation.

The Prophet also blessed me with a very real visit to my friend. Her body had been through a very traumatic experience physically and she was very weak and on bed rest. For a period of time she could not even ascend the stairs to her bedroom and had to sleep on her couch. I found myself as Soul sitting on the floor in her apartment and holding her hand while she lay on the couch. No words were spoken. The entire room was filled with a misty golden light, God's Love and Presence gently surrounding her and her family. Over her heart there was an intense pink light, which I believe to be God's healing

Light - the pink color to me represented an emotional healing filled with strength, love, and hope. Over her womb there was an intense orange light, which I believe represented physical healing, and strength to aid in repairing the physical trauma. God's Light and Love surrounded her and held her safe and sound. It gently but intensely washed over her and through her both physically and spiritually.

Words cannot fully convey the gift that this experience was and still is for me. In the year following her loss I am often taken back to this moment and I know she is still being nurtured and cared for by Our Heavenly Father. On the outer, I can support her with cards, phone calls, food, and honorary gifts in her daughter's name. Even more precious is the Divine opportunity to be able to pray to God to please, if it is His will, send strength, comfort, love, peace, healing, and even hope for a child in the future. God loves His children. And God loves when His children love one another.

My friend has again been blessed to conceive a child, this time a baby boy, due in October. He will learn all about his sister from those who love her. I am thankful to God for my lifelong friendship. I am thankful to God to know His

Light is real and powerful. I am thankful to the Prophet for showing me my friend being blessed with Divine Light as it brought me peace and comfort. I am thankful to know that God's Light brought a profound healing to her, whether or not she is fully aware of its magnitude.

Written by Catherine Hughes

30

Soul is Divine

Soul is an individualized piece of the Holy Ghost. We are not God, nor will we ever become God, but in a very real sense we are a piece of the Voice of God. This is the true meaning behind the statement of being created in the image of God. The more you come to accept this truth, the higher standard you will naturally seek to hold yourself to out of reverence for the Divinity within.

I woke early this morning to sit in contemplation and with appreciation for this beautiful day in the Light and Love of God. I surrender and declare myself a vehicle for God to be used in His service. I yield to the Divine and begin to sing HU, a beautiful prayer of love for God. The Prophet is with me and my heart fills with joy. While singing, I am taking note of the household's early morning activity. The cat jumps up next to where I sit. The dog is up; her nails clicking on the hard floors as she walks to the water bowl; a loud sound as she laps water. I am anticipating the sounds, which occur with the early morning routine as my husband rises to start his day. Not quite yet, but soon.

I continue to sing HU with love, which opens my heart. I notice I feel as if I am two beings. One, which is taking note and being distracted by the activity around me, and one which is singing HU with joy and love in my heart without being distracted by the activity around me. After a time, I feel the nudge to stop and just listen. A thought, "I yield to the Divine" comes in. I hear "You are Divine! You! Are! Divine!" I feel some strong emotion with those words, and I know I need to yield to myself, my higher self, which is my Divine self. And so the me in my Earth suit (my lower self), steps into my Divine suit (my higher self). I step in and pull my Divine suit on like a garment. It fits perfectly, forming exactly to my body like skin. I hold out one arm straight and run my other hand down it, admiring its qualities and how well it fits. It is made of light and it sparkles. I felt I was no longer two but one. The higher me. The Divine me, a child of God. I am so humbled, I get down to the floor on my knees with forehead to floor and stretch my arms straight out. Yielding to *THE* Divine. This beautiful Divine Light was all around, surrounding me. It is beautiful, filled with gold and it sparkles. Filling me inside and out, I felt as one with this beautiful Divine Light.

After a time, I become aware I am sitting once again, on my couch in my home. I open my eyes to the familiar, which surrounds me. But, I am different somehow. I am still feeling the warmth and the love of Divine Light, which is in me. Through this experience, the Prophet has given me a gift of peace and comfort. A feeling of being more relaxed and comfortable within myself. I was also blessed with a greater acceptance; a deeper knowingness of who I am and who we really are. We are Soul, and as Soul we are truly and literally a child of God, therefore we too are all Divine, even with our earthly challenges.

Written by Nancy Cumpston

31

Love of God is All Around

God's Love is the food of Soul. It is all around us shining through into our daily lives in numerous ways. There is no lack of Divine Love, it is simply a matter of learning to recognize it in all its forms. Most fortunate are those who have been given the eyes to see this love.

One evening as I prepared for bed after a day at the Nature Awareness School, I knelt in prayer by my sleeping bag and asked to more clearly see the many ways in which God's Love pours into my life and to help me accept more of it. Sometime later I awoke in a dream, and found that I was at my home, a few hours drive away from the school.

In this dream I was aware of my teacher standing next to me after he inwardly led me to my home. As I looked around I could clearly see that everything in my life is an expression of God's Love. I saw the smiles of my children and wife, the fruit trees in the yard and forest beyond, the furniture, house, and land; all these things are expressions of God's Love. As I looked around, seeing my usual surroundings in a new light, I perceived that all these everyday things of life sparkled with a golden light. The Prophet, my teacher, walked with me and showed me that all my relationships and all the objects in life, from cars to couches, from food to fresh water, are all available to me by the Grace of God, and are actual physical manifestations of the Light and Sound of God, the Love of God. I cannot say exactly how this information was conveyed to me, for I did not hear words spoken, but simply knew.

In this experience we even drove along my regular routes to the children's school and to my workshop and office. The way was paved with golden light. I could see there were no limits to the many forms of love, which are present in my life, and I am constantly surrounded by God's Love. It is present in a fixed, static form that comprises buildings and items, it comes through other loved ones in my life, and there is also a dynamic, flowing love which constantly pours forth into my heart, through the Prophet, from the very Heart of God.

So take a moment to look around your own life, and with Divine help and inspiration, see it all in a new light. There is no need to seek the Love of God, for you have this already in the measure you can accept today. With gratitude for the life we have today, let us draw nearer to God, and find a more abundant life tomorrow as God responds to our invitations, and draws nearer to us.

Written by Timothy Donley

32

Past Life and Promise of Healing

The Light of God can manifest in many different colors. Sometimes the specific color will provide additional insight into the experience. For example, many times orange light will accompany physical healing or insights into a past life. In the following example the author experiences both.

One of the ways that we grow as students of the Prophet, Del Hall, is to take his teachings home, integrate them into our lives, and go deeper. After a weeklong retreat this summer I invited his inner presence to join me for a HU song and contemplation. I had a soft intent to gain more information from the retreat and help myself with recurring neck and shoulder pain.

It was a beautiful Sunday morning and I was on my deck admiring the vegetable garden. We had just started harvesting some of the vegetables. It always amazes me what can grow from a tiny seed. I was reminded of the many seeds of truth Del had planted within my consciousness over the years that now bear fruit. The birds and insects were singing and I decided to join them. I began to sing HU, a love song to God. My heart was full of gratitude for my upcoming wedding. Although I was happy, my body was experiencing pain. I had tried numerous therapies for a few months, which brought temporary relief. This particular morning I remembered a spiritual exercise where we can ask our inner guide to bring God's healing orange Light to an area where we have illness or pain. I decided to do this during the quiet time after singing HU.

I had a strong awareness of the Prophet's inner presence with me. I became more tuned in to a sense that there was no separation between us. I was within the cosmic fabric that sustains everything. A strong reverence for the presence that encompassed me gave way to an orange effervescent light that cascaded over my being and into my physical body. It went to the source of pain, which unexpectedly became an impression of an arrow breaking through the left side of my upper shoulder from behind. This immediately sent a shooting nerve pain into my neck. It really hurt.

This was the recurring pain that I kept having off and on. Still deep in contemplation, I remembered that orange light is also one way God can reveal past lives to us. There was a lot of orange light in my inner vision. A name from a past life and time period came to me. I knew that I was not this particular person from the past, but the clue was that I was alive during this time in history and had sustained a battle wound in this area of my body. I had a vision of breaking the wooden shaft off where the arrow came through. I pulled the weapon out of my flesh. There was a sense of an infection that set in many days later and no more was revealed to me.

After this contemplation the pain that was there subsided. It had been dulled through this experience as if God's Prophet put a soothing balm on it. I was given a knowing that I need to be patient with this healing. It had many layers and would not be in my best interest at this time to simply fix the pain and move on. There was more to come over the year and I would get it as I could accept it. This lifetime was thousands of years back. I suppose I should have been more surprised at this but I wasn't. Anything is possible with God's Prophet. I can testify that he will do just about anything to help us (with our permission) to accept more of God's Love and more of our own Divinity. This is one of many occasions when I was given such grace.

I had been conditioned for this gift of love during the weeklong retreat I attended and frankly, over many lifetimes. Being taken back several thousand years was not random. The pain I was having wasn't random. It all ties into my personal journey over the years. There is a golden thread of love and truth that connects every experience I have and ever will have.

I was given a blessing with God's orange Light which brought insight into where my neck pain originated, temporary relief from the physical pain, and a knowingness that I am in the middle of a healing that is going to take more time to become permanent. It is a gift of love to be reassured of this, which brings greater trust throughout the process. I have come to learn that I have an easier time giving love than accepting it. With each healing from the past a greater ability to accept love has been given to me. The greatest joy I have found in life is the joy of giving. However, one can only give out what he or she can first accept.

I am so grateful to have learned some of the language of God. I know that many times colors of specific light are an expression of love, which contains infinite blessings.

Written by Tash Canine

33

Light of God Bathed Me

*Through the course of attending many retreats,
students receive help transitioning from operating in
the narrow human consciousness to the boundless one
of Soul. The more they operate as Soul, their eternal
spiritual side, the more of God's Light, Love, and truth
they can be witness to and accept. With the wisdom
and guidance of the Prophet there is no limit to this
potential for growth.*

Late one night at the Nature Awareness
School I had an incredible experience with the
Light and Sound of God. I was sitting on a bench
by the pond, savoring the moment and giving
thanks for all the blessings of the day. I watched
as several students from class went for a swim in
the pond after a guided spiritual exercise.
Something about them doing so was so beautiful
and sacred. As they emerged from the water I
saw them bathed in a golden light.

After everyone left there was a beautifully peaceful quiet and a stillness in the air. An "Oasis of Tranquility." I walked down to the pond's edge. As I approached, the water transformed right before me into a beautiful clear blue ocean. On the inner, the Prophet joined me on the beach. Gentle waves rolled in to greet us and invited me in. As I stepped in, the water felt alive, full of life, and had an indescribable feeling of love. This love cleansed, rejuvenated, and nourished me to my core. It contained everything I needed and would ever need! I can still feel this love deep in my heart to this day.

Even though it was night and physically dark outside, the water was illuminated with the intensity of a thousand suns. This would have been blinding to the human eye, yet I was not looking with my physical eyes. I was seeing with my spiritual eyes, as Soul. As Soul, we can travel with the Prophet through the Heavens to the God Worlds to have these experiences. The light I was seeing and experiencing was the Light of God. References to this Light can be found in the Bible. The entire area around me also resonated with the wondrous sound of the HU. All remembrances of time faded away. This sacred moment in eternity was more beautiful than anything I can describe with words.

The Prophet has taught me through years of personal experiences and loving guidance how to consciously operate more fully as my true self, Soul. Operating as Soul allows me to more deeply accept the love, grace, and blessings of God. When the Prophet brought me back from God's Ocean to the physical world I saw that I too had been bathed in God's golden Light and Love!

Each of these interactions with the Light or Sound of God has transformed me from the inside out. Each experience builds upon the ones before it. I have found that some of the blessings it has brought into my life are more love, peace, joy, wisdom, and abundance. God's Love affects and blesses everything it comes in contact with. This love blesses my family and I daily. I am so grateful for any and every experience with the Light and Sound of God through His Prophet. Thank you.

Written by Jason Levinson

34

Pink Healing Spiritual Light

It's a wonderful thing to be able to feel - to experience the emotions of living life here in the physical. However, if we let our emotions take charge they will run us ragged. The Light of God can help set us free by bringing us into balance with an emotional healing. Like all healing though, we must first truly be receptive for it to last.

The quality of my external life, a reflection of my emotional instability, reached a point where it had become unbearable. As a result of past mistakes in behavior and thought patterns I was full of remorse, guilt, and self-loathing. Thankfully, there was a light that still burned brightly deep inside the murky overlay of negativity I had heaped upon my true self. Soul; a spark of the Divine which when allowed to, burns brightly and fervently with God's Love.

By grace I was led to the Nature Awareness School and its founder, the Prophet Del Hall. He steadily, skillfully, and carefully helped me to chisel through the layers of untruth I was living and reveal a life of hope and worthwhile pursuits through which I would find peace and satisfaction. As I followed the Prophet's spiritual guidance and made change a priority, the truth I encountered slowly reformed and transformed me from the inside. My spiritual senses were becoming more refined.

One especially surprising gift of healing spiritual light came to me several years ago while I was readying myself for sleep after a long workday. It was a soothing pink glow that shown all about my bedroom. I blinked my eyes in amazement thinking that there was something wrong with my vision. The light remained for several minutes. I closed my eyes in contemplation and said a prayer of thanksgiving for this emotionally healing light of the Astral plane.

I am now aware that the gift of love that I received that night was not a singular event. It was the catalyst for the repair of my emotional body and the healing process still continues to heal emotional wounds, as I'm prepared to release them. My heart overflows with gratitude to God for the freedom that I now enjoy. My intention is to continue to follow the spiritual guidance of the Prophet so that I will be become all that I am born to be as a child of the Almighty.

Written by Bernadette Spitale

35

Journeys to the Fifth Heaven

*It is not quite as simple as "Heaven" and "Earth."
There are multiple levels to Heaven within the vast
worlds of God. Whether known as planes, realms,
spheres, mansions, or one of many other names, these
are real places. The Prophet is trained and authorized
to bring his students on spiritual journeys into the
various Heavens to gain in wisdom and understanding;
and how exciting it is.*

It was mid-March in the mountains when I attended a retreat held in a cozy log cabin. The trees were still bare, for it wasn't quite spring yet, but we students were beginning to unfold and grow like new spring leaves. We were just beginning to come into the realization of ourselves as Soul, and that we could be free from our cumbersome bodies to explore God's Worlds, guided and taken by God's Prophet.

One evening, as Del guided us in contemplation, I saw the Prophet in front of me and I took his offered hand. Together we slowly traveled up into the Heavens to the Astral plane, then to the Causal plane, to the Mental plane, and then to the Etheric plane, pausing along the way to meet other Prophets of old residing and teaching on those planes. When we reached the beginning of the fifth Heaven, the Soul plane, two Prophets greeted us. They each came next to me, one on either side and with the Prophet they brought me up into an amazing world of beautiful yellow light. As I looked around all was filled with the light. I felt so free, and so peaceful, since I was unencumbered by my physical body, and the distractions of my mind. It was still and quiet while I took in the beauty of the yellow light all around me. I looked at the Prophet; so excited and grateful to be there. I was also grateful for the two Prophets who helped me get there and the Prophets on the other planes who had appeared and welcomed me on each plane of the journey. This experience showed the possibilities of me as pure Soul with the Prophet. I wondered; if the Prophet of God could take me to a beautiful yellow world of light, what else is out there? My excitement grew to continue on this amazing journey to explore God's Worlds!

A year later, I had another opportunity to visit this beautiful world. When the experience began, I saw the Prophet in my inner vision and heard a high-pitched sound. As the sound became HU, the Prophet and I traveled up a column of this sound that appeared to be light flowing in gentle waves. Higher and higher we went, until we burst out of the lower worlds and into the Soul plane, the fifth Heaven. Again there was the feeling of peace and freedom and stillness as I looked all around me. This time I looked below me and I saw the beautiful purple light of the Etheric plane, the fourth Heaven below. It looked like a swirling galaxy of the most beautiful purple light I could ever imagine. I was awestruck as the Prophet and I floated there, looking down on the beautiful purple world below us.

My excitement continues to grow as I continue on this amazing journey, to learn about God's Worlds of Light and Love, but also importantly, I have learned about myself as Soul. I have learned to accept God's Love and to pass it on to others in many ways; and what a joy and a blessing it is to do so. Thank you Prophet for these exciting steps on my journey as Soul. I am grateful and excited as I look forward to the next step with you, for there is always more.

Written by Diane Kempf

36

Prayer for a Friend Answered

This is a touching story of witnessing a prayer for a friend being answered. The true pearl though is that we are heard. One of the greatest gifts we, as Soul, have been given is inner communication with God. The catch is, a lot a folks are not aware of or do not know how to develop it. One of the most important skills taught during our retreats is how to listen to, trust, and respond to this inner communication. This is part of teaching a man to fish versus handing him a fish.

Last year I had a friend who had a house fire. Although they did not lose much physically it was very hard on them emotionally and financially. They had to live in a small two-room hotel room (that is a small bedroom and a living/kitchen area) for over six months until all of the repairs were made to their house. This means two adults, two kids, a dog, and a cat in that two-room space for six months. This was a very stressful situation for the whole family and I was concerned for them. Before bed one night I said a prayer. I prayed to God that during this time they would find peace and love. I also asked the Divine for a dream to let me know that they were doing okay.

That night I had a dream about my friend that gave me much comfort and gratitude. I saw my friend and his family sitting on the bed in their small hotel room watching television. I was looking at them from the back of the room so they had their backs to me. They were all leaning in on one another and I could sense they were smiling. It looked like they were very happy together. We were not the only ones in the room though. There was a bright figure embracing them all. This bright figure was the Prophet sitting with them and embracing them all in his love and light. It was a moving experience to see this first hand. I am so grateful that I was allowed to be there and to know that they were truly doing okay. I thanked the Prophet for taking me on this journey. It is so wonderful to know that I can talk to God, be heard, and be answered.

Then a couple of weeks after the dream I felt as though I needed to do something more for him. I had a nudge to give some money to him that had been given to me. I found out that our office was raising donations for his family but I wanted him to know that this money had a special meaning to me. I had a fifty-dollar bill that had been given to me from Del, someone that I respect very much. I wanted to pay it forward. I waited until I could talk to him alone. I explained where the money had come from and that it meant a lot to me to be able to pass the money and the love that was with it on to him. As I handed it to him I said a quiet prayer for this to truly help him in some way. I believe that he could feel the love that was passed to him.

That night I again prayed that it would help him in whatever way was needed. Then, a couple of days later, he came to me with a big smile and explained that they had bought a couple of air mattresses with the fifty dollar gift for the kids to sleep on. He said that it was the first night since the fire that they had slept through the night. It made me feel so grateful that I was able to help by listening to the Divine on the inner and that I acted on what I was given. I am so thankful that I was able to be a conduit to pass along some of God's Love to him and his family. Since I started attending spiritual retreats I have learned to listen to my nudges and see the truth in my dreams. This has truly brought more peace and love into my life.

Written by Anthony Allred

37

Ring of Light

There is a period of introduction after the seeker first meets the Prophet and begins his spiritual studies - a time of getting to know each other. Eventually though, the seeker must make a commitment to the path, the teacher, and the teachings because it's hard to enjoy the freedom of sailing if you still have one foot on the dock. Getting in the boat is a personal choice and one that should be motivated by love.

In 2010 I attended a weeklong spiritual retreat at Nature Awareness School. Del Hall, the Prophet, led our class in a spiritual travel experience to a Temple of God at the twelfth Heaven. After we sang HU we were taken by the Prophet, our inner guide, to a special place of our choosing anywhere in the temple. The Prophet and I were on a terrace where we sat down at a small table. He said that he had a gift that he wanted to give to me.

He presented me with a small box that was the kind that holds a ring. As he opened the box, light began to pour out of the edges of the box until it was fully opened. Inside of the little box was a ring made of light. He put the ring on my ring finger, which already had my wedding ring on it, and the ring of light covered my physical wedding ring. The ring was so bright I could hardly see my fingers. This was a very special and personal gift and I was immediately grateful.

I later contemplated on the meaning of the gift of the ring of light. I began to realize that it represents my spiritual marriage to the Prophet. It took awhile for me to understand the true meaning of this personal gift. I believe the Prophet knew that I had become serious about my spiritual studies. After this experience I more fully and on a deeper level accepted the Prophet as my guide for my spiritual journey home to God.

Finding balance between my lower physical self and my true self, Soul, now began in earnest. I was now in a sacred spiritual marriage and wanted to grow and do my part. This realization brought to light for me that I had been using too much energy pursuing worldly thoughts and actions, which usually yielded more earthly troubles. I learned to strengthen my relationship with the Prophet on the inner and to include him in all my life's activities and decisions. After I sing HU I often sing "Prophet" for a few minutes. This began to put more balance into my life. Throughout the day I knew that the Prophet was with me spiritually, I could feel his presence with me. I began to share my thoughts and ask for his suggestions. Over time I began to understand his feedback to my questions and knew he was sharing a higher view of life that could bless and guide me.

It took some time for me to grow into the perspective that everything is spiritual and cannot be separated from God. Every now and then I look at my ring finger and envision this ring of light, because it represents my commitment as Soul, a child of God. I am enjoying my journey home to God with the Prophet and my daily physical life more than ever.

Written by Sam Spitale

38

I Heard Heavenly Music

Within the Heavenly realms the Voice of God, or the Holy Ghost, manifests itself in a wide range of spiritual light and sound. Often the color of the light, or in the following case the sound heard, is a road mark of sorts to which Heavenly plane Soul is on. God delivers His Love to Soul via the light and sound, so to experience the Voice of God in any form is a profound blessing.

Throughout my spiritual studies I had oftentimes read about the beautiful sounds that can be heard on the various spiritual planes of existence. In my heart I desired that I might have an experience of hearing Heavenly music, but it was not forthcoming until just recently. On June 7, 2015 many gathered in singing HU; a love song to God, in the presence of the Prophet Del Hall. I began by letting go of all external distractions. I prayed to become a perfect vehicle for God's Love, all the while opening my heart to allow a continuous stream of God's Love to flow through it with each wave of HU.

There was a sense of being lifted up spiritually higher as we continued to send love out to the unseen worlds. We had been singing for about ten minutes when, within the sound of those singing HU, I distinctly heard the sound of a flute. Elated about the blessing of hearing the sound of the fifth Heaven, the Soul plane, my heart soared with love as I sang to my Heavenly Father. More sound came into my awareness; it was of violins, the sound that originates on the eighth spiritual plane. I now had personally been blessed to experience the Holy Ghost, God's Voice, as both light and sound!

I was allowed to experience these sounds in order that I might testify to the reality of Soul's ability to travel in worlds beyond what the physical eye can see. I also know that to experience God's Light or Sound is a special gift of love. Since I was singing in the presence of the Prophet of God, there was a plus factor at play that one will only know by direct experience.

In appreciation of and gratitude for the blessings!

Written by Bernadette Spitale

39

Best Christmas Gift Ever

Christmas is a time to celebrate the love God has for us.
We are each known, guided home, and loved personally
by God. This love can come to us in many ways. One of
the most direct is to experience God's Light in your inner
vision or in the physical itself. The following is a beautiful
example of the latter. What better Christmas gift than
being comforted by the Divine.

I was walking on the beach while visiting family on Long Island, on Christmas Day, 2013. Although I was having a relatively good time and enjoying their company, there was a loneliness that I had been experiencing for a period of time. The ups and downs of everyday life, as well as having no significant other to share them with, had led to a low-grade melancholy that I think I was not even fully aware of.

It was late afternoon and the sunset was drawing near. I started to become aware of a distinctly different pattern in the sky, and in all my years of experiencing sunsets, I had never seen anything like it before. There was a beam of light in the sky coming directly down from the Heavens. This beam was golden and perfectly vertical, as if someone had literally carved it out of the clouds behind it. At the bottom the light fanned out and spread across the land and sea in great golden waves.

As I stood there and watched in awe it became more and more distinct. It did not change or dissipate. On the contrary, it was as if time stood still. Everything became very quiet. The amount of light seemed to stay the same even though it was dusk and night was falling. The colors and patterns in the sky were suspended. There was not a breath of wind. And although it was a very cold day, I ceased to be cold.

I stood enveloped in the pure peace and stillness of God's Love, and as my spiritual guide Del has taught me over the years, one of the ways to recognize the presence of the Divine is in the form of a beam or column of light. I have experienced this beam of light many times in my inner spiritual experiences, so I had already been conditioned to recognize the gift when it manifested physically. I knew very well that I was having a full-blown experience with the Light of God.

There were many gifts and treasures that came along with, and remained in the afterglow of, this sacred experience with the Divine. And probably many more that I cannot even begin to fathom. The following day I continued to feel God's Presence very strongly – and perhaps deeper than ever before; it was more a part of me and I more a part of it. That presence was in my consciousness at every turn. I experienced a great many things at once; a combination of gratitude, awareness, love, trust, balance, clarity, and deep, deep peace. It was as if I had literally received a download of Divine attributes.

As I prepared to write about this experience I found myself returning to it and reliving it on a deeper level. I had insights and awareness that I had not even been conscious of before. I realized I was not simply remembering or recalling something; I was re-experiencing something that is alive and fluid, and still available to nourish and uplift me at any time.

Perhaps one of the greatest pearls of this experience is how personal my relationship with the Divine is. God knew my heart was heavy, even more than I did, and personally gave me a gift of love, hand-delivered, on Christmas Day. He reminded me that when I am fully immersed in His Presence there is nothing else I need. Although I still have ups and downs in my life, I am forever changed from the experience. The bar has forever been raised on what is possible and attainable for me spiritually, and for any one of God's children who has the genuine desire to connect with him.

Written by Laurence Elder

40

The Gift of the Golden Leaf

It is hard for some to accept that we are each known and loved personally by God. The Divine constantly showers us with this love in very specific ways. God's Love comes in ways that are special to us - in forms we can recognize and accept. Once you learn the "Language of the Divine" you will see and feel this love everywhere.

As a kid, walking to and sitting on this old familiar bench that overlooked the Hudson River was a place where I found peace. I visited this bench many times over the course of my life right up into my twenties.

In November, I attended a spiritual class at the Nature Awareness School. Shortly after our group HU sing I sat on a bench that overlooked the pond. As I sat peace filled my heart, and then I had a memory of seeing the sun's reflection in that same pond five years earlier. It was the sun I saw, but it was more than the sun; it was an overwhelming reflection of God's Light and Love.

As I continued to sit and remember and re-experience, I noticed a single white oak leaf floating on the pond. It was brilliantly red and completely surrounded by the color blue. Then the red turned to orange and then to gold, and it was a gold that I have never seen here on Earth before. It was the most beautiful leaf that I have ever seen; a symbol to me of God's Presence and Love. This sight gave me more peace and such joy, and my heart was singing. It was a gift just for me and I instinctively knew it. God has used leaves before as a way to get my attention, and again He was letting me know I am not alone, and that I am loved.

Written by Moira Cervone

41

Love the Lord With all Your Heart

The simple but profound truth is, you exist because God loves you. It is one thing to have someone tell you this - it is quite another to have a spiritual guide who can help you come to know this truth for yourself. Joy and abundance beyond measure are available when you personally experience God's Love.

Luke 10:27 – "And he answering said, Thou shalt love the Lord thy God with all thy heart, and with all thy soul, and with all thy strength, and with all thy mind; and thy neighbor as thyself."

My fervent prayer as a child and young adult was to truly know that God loves me and how to love God, not just in my mind. I wanted to come before God through love, not through fear and guilt that many churches promote. One of my very favorite passages in the Bible was about loving God with all your heart, mind, and Soul. This passage has been tucked away in my heart. It always was clear to me that one of Jesus' key messages was that God, His Father, is love and how much we are loved and the importance of loving others as ourselves. In everyday life I had a hard time loving myself and was harder on myself than others. Not being able to love myself it was difficult to accept God's Love, though it was always there for me. This sense of unworthiness dogged me much of my life.

In 1998 I was guided to the Nature Awareness School. Over the years my spiritual teacher, who is a true Prophet of God, gradually guided me through every angle possible, a 360-degree view, to experience how much I am loved, and that I am worthy of God's Love. God loves us all, every one of us unconditionally. I learned that we are here on Earth to learn about giving and receiving love. I learned and began to experience the amazing inner joy of reaching out to others, instead of only thinking about myself.

A priceless experience was gifted to me a few years ago; one I treasure and hope to remember in my heart forever. It took place shortly after one of my friends, also a student of Del's, had shared a facilitation at a retreat that was full of love. There was a sense of expectant joy in the air as Del returned to the front of the room. The Prophet suggested, "Let's come together, be really together for a moment. Let go; surrender with the inner Prophet's assistance." I/we merged into a gigantic white light ball which got brighter and brighter. I was aware of the particles of light, sparks of individuality within the greater light ball (God's Light). "In this moment you have everything you need." And I felt my cares, everything melt away. And the more I surrendered, let go, the boundaries of various boxes that had contained my limited concept of God faded away and my awareness of the limitlessness and expansiveness of the gigantic white light ball grew and grew.

"Just be." I experienced a stillness, deep peace, and Divine Love. I felt totally nourished in that moment of eternity and had everything I needed. As the love became more intense, I accepted it, almost overpowering, and felt so much love for God. The flow back and forth between God's Heart and my heart intensified until it became a crescendo of golden waves of love crashing upon the shores of my heart. My heart was bursting with love for God. In that moment of eternity, I only wanted to love and praise God forever. In that moment as Soul I experienced my favorite Bible passage... "to love the Lord God with all my heart, mind, and Soul."

Written by Jan Reid

42

God's Healing Love

God's Light and Love give us life - we are never without them. We were created from and continue to be nourished and sustained by God's Light and Love. However, when we take steps to draw closer to God we can experience them in ever-greater magnitudes. There is no ill that the Light of God cannot sooth.

One morning I awoke early feeling quite poorly with a headache accompanied by nausea. Since I worked the afternoon shift I decided that there was sufficient time to allow the sick feeling to go away on its own, instead of taking medication. Several hours passed without any relief. I decided to prepare for a short nap with a spiritual practice that brings me peace and comfort. I opened my heart and expressed love and appreciation to my creator by singing HU, then went to sleep. HU is a love song to God that was taught to me by the Prophet Del Hall, my spiritual teacher.

While I was asleep I had a dream of being bathed in a beautiful and comforting golden light. Upon awakening the symptoms of my illness were completely gone. Gratitude for the healing Light of God's Love overtook me while I realized how much I am loved and cared for.

The Prophet has taught me how to fortify my awareness of the connection that exists between my creator and me. He has helped me to recognize that the personal love connection that I have with the Divine is the most precious bond that I will ever have.

Written by Bernadette Spitale

43

A Child of God is Born

Sometimes God pulls back a curtain allowing us to experience the spirituality of a situation. The following is a beautiful testimony of witnessing the sacredness of childbirth. It is at this moment that Soul enters the body and a new adventure begins.

How grateful I am for my children, three gifts that God has bestowed upon my wife and I. What were once happy "additions" to the family are now integral parts that I would not want to imagine our lives without. Each of my children's births was a precious and sacred moment, but it was the birth of my eldest child that gave me a glimpse into the Divinity that was clothed in each little bundle of joy.

The morning my oldest child was born, I stood in the delivery room experiencing all the nervousness and excitement of a first-time dad-to-be. My mind raced forwards and backwards as the moment crawled nearer and nearer.

Because I was at the front of the bed, ready to offer sips of water and cold washcloths to my wife, I could see everyone else in the room. Several people, including the doctor, head nurse, and various other nurses and assistants popped in and out. Time seemed to slow to a freeze and I watched, with this sort of detached viewpoint, a panorama of the other people there.

There was what I can only describe as a reverent anticipation bubbling up in the room. Everyone - it seemed like a lot more than the three or four individuals there - seemed riveted on this sacred moment. There was an overwhelming reverence for Soul permeating the air. A spark of God was about to don another body, take its knocks, learn its lessons, and continue on Its journey home to the Heart of God. I believe each person there, whether conscious of it or not, was recognizing Soul – the Divine spark about to be housed in a tiny little body - but also which lived in each other and in themselves. Each in his or her own way recognized that the source of this spark of life was God.

While my wife, the doctor, and several nurses prepared for the imminent birth, a young nursing assistant stood in the middle of the room unconsciously rocking back and forth, in a slow cadence to some distant rhythm only she could hear. She hugged herself instinctively, as if rocking an invisible baby in her arms. It was hard to say if she was imagining comforting the baby about to be born or herself. Maybe both.

When my son finally arrived, I moved into position to "catch" him. I witnessed a ball of glowing light so intense and brilliant it became hard to see anything else. I immediately recognized this Soul as someone I had loved dearly before. Watching Soul enter the body was breathtaking. The doctor and nurses helped guide his tiny body into my arms. I was holding him when he took his first breath in this body, before surrendering him to my wife's welcoming embrace. The recognition between mother and son seemed apparent as well.

In my years at the Nature Awareness School, Del has repeatedly led me to experiences that have shown me there is so much more to us than just our bodies – much more than just the parts we can normally see. I believe I witnessed a glimpse of that in my son as he was being born, a glimpse into the Divine essence of our being which is born into this world to learn, to love, and to attempt to pick up the trail back to Its eternal Home.

Written by Chris Comfort

44

Purple Light of God

When viewed from the perspective of Soul you have a single lifetime to live; for Soul is eternal, it lives forever. However, Soul incarnates many many times within a new physical body to continue its journey of learning more about giving and receiving love. Along the way Soul picks up likes and dislikes from the myriad of experiences it has. Consciously, we may not remember our previous lives, but they have helped shape who we are today. If it is in our best spiritual interest the Prophet will reveal a past life to us. When this is the case, it is done to help us with something in this lifetime.

Have you ever struggled to appreciate the job that you have, or any blessings that are already in your life? I certainly have, and it is my prayer that this short story may help you to appreciate how a relationship with the Prophet of God can bring both abundance and freedom into your life. When I first arrived for a class at the Nature Awareness School twenty-one years ago, I did not appreciate the gift that God had given me in this lifetime of living in a country that protected our God-given rights of freedom, of religion, and of speech. Nor had I been grateful for the work that I had, which had often consisted of outdoor labor on farms. The experience of being in the presence of Del, the true Prophet of God, and applying in daily life what he taught me at numerous classes with him, over time, changed my attitude towards life to one of gratitude for the blessings that fill it constantly. Among the key principles that Del taught in my early years of study at the school were those of gratitude being the secret of love and that our real identity is that of Soul. I learned that, as Soul, I am an eternal being that has operated many bodies over the course of one incarnation after another.

During a HU sing that Del led, I was blessed with an experience that helped me to more fully appreciate these principles along with the gift of living here in the state of Virginia. As we were singing this ancient name for God, the inner Prophet gave me a vision of a scene from a movie that I watched as a kid by the name of "America, America." It was a scene at the end of the movie in which a Greek immigrant who had gone through a long, arduous journey to reach the United States finally arrives on American soil at Ellis Island, in New York City. He is clearly excited to have reached his new home as the movie ends. As I viewed this scene, a wave of gratitude for my life here in the United States, a country that many have struggled long and hard to get to, washed through me. A while later, during this same HU sing, the spiritual presence of the Prophet took me to a scene that I recognized as being in rural Virginia. My heart filled with gratitude for Thomas Jefferson and what he did to create the country that I now live in, and then suddenly my spiritual eye became filled with the purple Light of God. For a beautiful, long moment, all that I could see was this beautiful purple light. I felt this deep gratitude for a past lifetime in Virginia. This gratitude included the feeling that I had spent a lot of my time in hard physical labor on a farm or plantation some two hundred years ago when Jefferson was alive, and that it was a gift to me to serve in this way.

In this experience I was not only grateful for the freedoms that Jefferson helped secure for the country that I live in, but also for the beauty of the landscape that he created. At the time that I was given this experience, I had not fully appreciated the gift of having a job landscaping at the university that Jefferson founded. I appreciated this gift more after receiving this blessing of the Light and Love of God. Gratitude is gratitude, whether it is for the country one lives in, a feeling about a past life, or gratitude for a job. Gratitude opens the heart to receiving more Divine Love. Service is service, whether it is service through writing a document that declares our right to live in freedom or doing manual labor with love in your heart for the job that you do. This experience with the Light of God is one of so many gifts of love from the Prophet that have helped me to appreciate the blessings already in my life. These blessing have included years working at a job that provides for my basic needs in a state that I loved dearly in a past lifetime and am blessed to return to again in this lifetime.

Among the many truths that Del has taught me is that the purple light is a form of communication between God and Soul that is beyond the world of the analytical, logical mind. The logical mind, that I had valued so much at one time, could never make sense of feelings about a past life, or that it was a gift to be able to serve through hard physical labor. Soul, our true identity, lives beyond the limitations of the mind and is able to look deeper into the true meaning of life than the mind can ever do. I experienced true Divine Love within that purple light, along with gratitude for a past-life connection to the country that I live in now, a connection that helps me to appreciate the abundance of blessings in my life today. Among these blessings is the freedom to write this story about a spiritual experience with God's Light and His Prophet without concern that I will be imprisoned for writing something that is not within the boundaries of conventional religious doctrine. An even greater freedom that I have been blessed with, thanks to my relationship with the Prophet, is the freedom to recognize my true nature as Soul, an eternal being that is blessed with God's Love and His Light.

Written by Roland Vonder Muhll

45

God's Love in My Home

God's Light and Love is everywhere. The farther we travel on the path, the greater amount of this love the Prophet can share with us and help us to accept. Sometimes the daily challenges of life cause us to lose sight of this miracle. It is however the remembrance and appreciation of God's Love in our life that blesses us, and those we come in contact with.

During one of the classes at the Nature Awareness School Del led us on a guided experience into the inner worlds. The Prophet, my inner teacher and spiritual guide, appeared on the screen of my inner vision. He opened his heart and shared his love. I could feel this love, God's Love, pouring into me. He asked us to stretch and take in more love. I felt myself growing from the inside out with more love than I can ever remember feeling. We were asked to stretch again and take in more love. I continued to stretch and grow with love. The Prophet expressed how much love he wanted to share with us and I could feel this as he shared. I saw myself stretching and stretching with all that Divine Love. I was filled with so much love to the point of bursting.

We were asked to travel via the inner worlds to our homes. We were to recognize all around our homes reminders of this moment and of God's Love. The Prophet and I traveled to my home and as I started looking, I could see this love. God's Love was everywhere in my home. I moved around and touched the places that meant the most to me. I saw that it was God's Love that brought these things into my life.

As I touched and recognized these gifts, golden light appeared and remained, a reminder of these incredible blessings. Going all around my home, both inside and out, I saw God's wonderful Love in everything I held dear. Golden light reminders appeared in my home, in my studio, in the barn, and in the yard. I was reminded that every time I would use, touch, see, or think about these things I would see God's golden Light and experience God's Love. I pictured myself driving to work and interacting at the office, and experiencing this love all along the way. As that experience concluded, I looked forward to seeing all those reminders on the property when I returned home.

After the class ended, I drove home and upon turning down the gravel road, huge ruts and washouts crisscrossed the driveway from rainstorms that occurred while I was away. These needed immediate attention and I felt some stress building. I was scheduled to travel very early the next morning and still had to prepare and pack. I now had several hours of hard labor ahead of me to repair the driveway. Gathering up the pick, rakes, and shovels I felt a bit grumpy as I started filling in the ruts. Suddenly like a bolt out of the blue, I was reminded of all the love God has blessed me with. I could see those reminders of golden light all around, even on the driveway where I was working. I started laughing at myself for being so short sighted. I expressed my love and gratitude by singing HU, thanking God for the wonderful gifts of Divine Love that had been given just days before. What a gift to see and experience this once again! What a blessing to see those reminders, and to experience that love as I now repaired the driveway with joy in my heart.

Written by Paul Nelson

46

Witnessing the Voice of God

The experiences we are blessed to have with God, the Prophet, and the Holy Spirit build our trust in the Divine and provide "food for Soul." If they are not only written in our journals, but rather etched in our hearts, we can relive them multiple times and they will continue to provide spiritual nourishment.

The Prophet is a Divinely inspired teacher who speaks the Word of God. I have witnessed numerous sacred experiences over the years that solidify my trust in the Prophet. He has guided me through my life and because of this my life has become so abundant with joy, love, clarity, truth, and so many more of the glories of God. Out of all the experiences I have had that build my trust and faith in the Prophet, this is one that really stands out.

I was blessed to see, with my physical eyes, the Prophet speaking as the Voice of God, speaking the true Word of God. I watched as he spoke during a retreat at the Nature Awareness School and I saw what I can only describe as the Light of God flowing straight from his mouth. With each word he spoke a beautiful golden light streamed directly from his mouth. The Word of God was manifesting. I blinked my eyes a few times to make sure I was seeing clearly. This was amazing; I could actually see the Light of God physically coming from the Prophet's mouth as he was speaking the Word of God.

Re-living this experience continues to amaze me. I am so grateful to have been blessed with an experience similar to those written about in scripture. Being witness to this has fortified my loving relationship with the Prophet.

Written by Emily Allred

47

Tea With the Prophet

One of the most sacred things to understand about the Prophet is his ability to teach you in the physical - the "outer" and in the spiritual realms, or the "inner." By connecting with us, in both these states, more wisdom and joy can be passed on and in a very real sense, we are never alone.

The Prophet is always with me. Throughout the day, in everything I do, his loving presence is there to guide me. To consult with and to share all the ups and downs, interactions, and experiences that flow in and out of my life. Our relationship is sacred and it is the most precious gift ever.

Sometimes after a long bustling day, I like to sit and enjoy a hot cup of tea and just be quiet. Even though I know he is there, I don't want to take his presence for granted, so I'll consciously invite the Prophet to share a cup of tea with me.

There is something beautiful and very special about sitting in silence with someone you love.

One frigid night this past winter as we sat having tea, listening to the crackling of the fire, I was feeling especially grateful for its warmth. I was also appreciating the gifts of health to cut the wood that was burning, a warm home, the kitty curled up on my lap, knowing who the Prophet is, and being able to share this time together. I began to sing HU. HU is a love song to God and in singing HU, I was expressing my love and saying "Thank you for all this abundance."

The Prophet took me to a place in the inner spiritual worlds that is peaceful, calm, and very still. There was no time and no movement. It just was, and it was exquisite. It was like an oasis of tranquility. My whole being smiled and was filled with joy as I listened to the Sound of Divine Spirit, the sweet music of the Heavens. Its life-giving energy flowed through me. I rested there with the Prophet and was nourished and rejuvenated.

A unique ability God gives the Prophet is that he can be with someone on the inner and the outer; both are important to one's spiritual growth. Whether conscious of it or not, we are never alone and never have been. But if we invite the Prophet into our heart and nurture that relationship, life will be blessed in ways beyond imagination and dreams can become reality. His love (that has always been there) can flow more freely; inspiring and uplifting us and every aspect of our life. Life lived with the Prophet makes ordinary things extra-ordinary and can turn a simple cup of tea into a sacred experience to savor and cherish.

Written by Lorraine Fortier

48

Orange Light on a Past Life

Any desire for healing or spiritual growth that does not take past lives into consideration is building on a partial foundation. You are at this moment the sum of all your experiences from all your lifetimes. Thus, a true spiritual healing needs to have a broader scope than a single lifetime - it must go to the root.

During a recent contemplation at a class at the Nature Awareness School, I found myself in an orange-lit world. Del, a true Prophet of God, was inviting us to meet with the Prophet from the time period over two thousand years ago, as we were then. In many lifetimes we are not aware of the Prophet. He is always with us whether we realize it or not. In some lifetimes we may meet the Prophet of the time in his physical presence. Those encounters always affect us even if we do not realize it at the time. In other lifetimes we may be consciously aware of him. In the real "gift lifetimes" he is our teacher, and we can nurture a relationship with both the physical and the inner spiritual part of him. During this contemplation I was aware of the Prophet from those old times. I saw his robe and part of his face. Mostly I was aware of his holy presence. Because I was also being bathed in spiritual orange light I knew this could be a past life experience. That meant the Prophet had taken me to the third Heaven where memory patterns and histories from our past lifetimes are stored. Since the orange light was visible, this particular lifetime with the former Prophet may be significant for me.

There is another aspect of the orange light. It is associated sometimes with physical healing. Present physical ailments may be the result of past life choices or experiences, though not always. Del has stated that there really is no need to know of a past life unless it can help us live a better life now. Soul lives in the present. Through many years of being in the physical presence of the current Prophet and through our ongoing inner relationship, I have received blessings of physical or emotional healings. In this experience with a very special Prophet of that time and because I was bathed in orange light let me know that it was a significant lifetime for me. I felt I received a healing that I needed to live this life more fully. I am grateful for this lifetime, being allowed and guided by that former Prophet to be taught by the current Prophet, and having a relationship of love and trust with both.

During another class, the Prophet led us in a discussion that went deeper than we had before regarding healings, which all of us had been blessed to experience so many times. An analogy of tuning a guitar was used. A guitar can be tuned, but if there is a kink anywhere in a guitar string, the guitar can never really be tuned quite correctly or for very long until the kink is taken out or the string replaced. Each fret on the neck of the guitar represents a past life in this example. The Causal plane, where there is often orange light, may have a memory pattern or a karmic record. If the guitar string is kinked at a certain fret, a past life, it can affect all future lives in a negative way. A kink could represent a hurt, sorrow, sadness, misunderstanding, or even a physical injury that is still the root of a current illness or pain. Though we may receive many healings, until we receive and accept, the healing from the old lifetime, it will be difficult to rise up to a higher viewpoint consistently and permanently. In other words, God through His Prophet can heal issues from our past, today!

Lifetime after lifetime can occur with little or insignificant change to enslaving patterns, such as fear, guilt, lack of confidence, ignorance, among others, before Soul has the opportunity to consciously meet the Prophet and develop a relationship. A greater freedom, which may be manifested as more joy, peace, making good choices in life, clarity, better health, and more comes at God's timing as the Prophet works at the right pace for each Soul to untangle an old kink in a guitar string.

Written by Martha Stinson

49

Shackled to Ball and Chain

Your ability to grow spiritually is directly proportional to your ability to accept truth. This can be more difficult when it is about yourself and not flattering. However, if you wish to be freed of the things holding you back you have to first be able to accept they are there. The truth will set you free.

About a year and a half ago, I had a life changing healing by God's Grace. For several months I had been in a funk. I knew something was off but I did not know what it was or how to fix it. I wanted to make changes in my life – switching jobs, moving, etc. I was caught up in thinking only about myself and my actions were reflecting my self-indulgence. Spiritually, I was lazy and acting like a juvenile. I was spinning my wheels spiritually and felt like I was stuck. When you stop moving forward spiritually you cannot stay in one place; you tend to slide backwards. That is exactly what I was doing. I was allowing negative thoughts into my consciousness and these were turning into a self-fulfilling prophecy.

During a class at the Nature Awareness School my teacher lovingly pointed out to me how I had allowed my foggy thinking to get me "into a real pickle." He gave me a lot of truth about myself and with God's help, I was able to hear the truth and begin to accept it. The clear truth from my teacher was an answer to a prayer that had been in my heart. Even though I was not fully aware of how much of a mess I had created with my negative thoughts, I knew I needed help from the Divine and God read my heart.

After class was over for the evening, I walked down to the pond and sat on a bench. I sang HU for a while and begged for the Divine to help me learn this lesson, see more clearly, and begin moving forward spiritually again. I wanted to overcome this "hiccup" and put it in the past. When I stopped talking I then saw a shackle around my neck, with a long chain and a ball attached to it. I saw the bright white Light of God around me, and then it became more intense and focused. It looked like a laser beam. The laser beam of God's Love burned through the shackle that was around me and I was released. I surrendered whatever the ball and shackle represented to the Divine and knew that I had been given a gift from God. If I were to focus on that shackle and feel bad for whatever it was it would have been counterproductive and self-indulgent.

I still do not know to this day what the shackle was and I am fine with that. By the Divine Grace of God, I was free. God read my heart and also heard my prayer that night. I am no longer caught up by my foggy thinking and am spiritually growing and moving forward again.

Thank you God for hearing all of my prayers and answering those in my best interest.

Written by Michelle Kempf

50

The Flute of Heaven

My father has led many a seeker on journeys into the Heavenly realms during both waking and sleeping states to experience the Holy Ghost - the Sound and Light of God. These travels help shed light on your true nature as a spiritual being and pull back the curtain on the Heavenly Kingdom.

When I was a young boy my parents played traditional Japanese flute music each night to help me fall asleep. The gentle melodies seemed to be the only thing that could coax me into rest. The soothing compositions brought a peace that was largely absent during my waking hours. I looked forward each night to the familiar sounds. I am so grateful that they played this beautiful music. But nothing could compare to the music of the flute I heard in a dream, years later.

This dream was given to me seven years ago. I awoke in full consciousness to find myself in a region of pure light. As far as the eye could see was vibrant, pulsating, yellow light emanating from a central figure. Closer to the figure the light became ever more pure, whiter and whiter, finer and finer. The light itself seemed dynamic and alive. In the middle of this light-filled universe sat Del Hall, my spiritual guide, a true Prophet of God. He played a traditional wooden flute.

His music filled this world, the most beautiful sound I have ever heard! As he played, I did not know if a minute had passed, or a day, or a month, or a year. I could not tell distance either: Del sat in the center of this beautiful world, but was he three feet away, or three miles? There was no way to tell, for there was no matter in this realm. It was only the pure Light and Sound of Heaven. As he played, the music brought peace that far surpassed anything I had experienced before. This peace entered me and filled me, and it lives in my heart to this day. It is a gift that keeps on giving. Simply placing my attention on this dream brings back the serenity of this beautiful music. This is the peace that surpasses all understanding, spoken of in the Bible. Upon waking, I was overcome and gave thanks for this incredible experience.

This was more than a dream. It was a journey into Heaven. The fifth Heaven, where only purity and goodness and light exist. There was no time, no near or far, no shadow, no high or low. There was only the Source, and the Light and Sound of God. In the Bible, Saint Paul said he knew a man who was caught up to the third Heaven (Second Corinthians 12:2). This means that there is at least a first Heaven, a second, and a third. This dream took place in the fifth Heaven, where there is no matter, only spiritual light and sound. There is no evil, only goodness and light. As a Prophet of God, Del Hall is able to take his students into the Heavens in full consciousness. To the fifth Heaven and beyond.

This dream motivated me to continue my spiritual path without hesitation. It showed me that Del was no *ordinary* preacher or spiritual teacher. Something I had already known in my heart, but this left no doubt. He is the modern Prophet of God, able to share the Light and Sound of God. Following his teachings and guidance had led to this experience, and the understanding of it.

Many have heard references to the Light of God. Few have heard of the Sound, the Heavenly white music. Yet scattered references to it exist in the various world scriptures. Having experienced it, I can tell you that it is unlike anything else. It is more than "music." It is the Voice of God, and it carries all the qualities of God's Love. Peace, love, mercy, joy, and more! It can be experienced by man today. It is this sound, this beautiful Sound of God that can carry Soul back to its eternal home.

Written by David Hughes

51

A Sky Full of Love

*God uses His Light as a major way to deliver blessings
to Soul. The light may come to us in the dream state,
during prayer, or contemplation, while spiritually
traveling, or in the following example, in the waking
state. The more we are blessed to experience the Light
of God, the more conditioned we become to accepting
the blessings contained within the light. One of which,
is comforting us through lifting sadness from our heart.*

Psalm 19:1 – "The heavens declare the glory of God, and the sky above proclaims his handiwork."

In the fall of 1997 I was driving the fifty-minute commute to my new job. As I did each morning, I sang HU the entire way into the city. Not an innate morning person, I appreciated the peaceful time to express my love directly to God. It was a time of great change in my life. It was one of those transitional periods where a relationship, job, and living arrangements all had recently ended. Everything was wide open, new, and uncertain. It was an amazing opportunity to put more of my trust and focus from the changing temporal world and onto the solid foundation of the Divine.

My experiences at the Nature Awareness School had blessed me with seeing the Light of God many times. At the school in the presence of my spiritual teacher, Del Hall, I experienced this light many times. Flashes of pink, bursts of blues and orange, beams of white and gold. As my spiritual strength and endurance developed under his guidance, so did the length, clarity, and intensity of the light I experienced.

The common thread at this time was that my experiences with the Light of God all occurred at the Nature Awareness School in the presence of Del. Though I spent several weekends a year there, most of the year was lived off the mountain. And that life was surely in need of the Light of God! It is impractical for the Prophet to be with you physically everywhere. But spiritually you can be aware of his presence throughout your day and in doing so, invest in your relationship with God through one of His living Prophets, whom He always blesses us with here on Earth.

So that morning as I drove into the city I experienced a mixture of sadness and hope, wondering about my place in God's great creation. Where was I heading? I wondered. What was God's plan for me, and for my life? The morning sky was slowly transitioning from dark to light – a metaphor for my life the two years I had been coming to the school. The sun was just waking, the colors of the day beginning to stir.

Suddenly the sky filled with the purest blue light. It was not an everyday, afternoon blue sky. It was startling. It stretched like blue fire from horizon to horizon. It surrounded me in a bubble of grace and warmth. I had seen the sky fill with supernatural blue light once before on a farm – years before I started coming to the school. That was also during a time of great transition. It tugged at my heart then as it did now, but I had not been conditioned to accept the amount of love present in the light. It had opened my heart and soothed me, but I did not recognize the holy Presence of God and the unconditional love that was there for me.

Fortunately the road I was on was a highway, a straight road with few cars at this time and no traffic lights. I continued to HU. The sky again filled with blue. I recognized this as the Prophet's presence. Though not limited to it, the color blue is often the spiritual calling card of the Prophet of the times. As the sky filled I felt my heart fill with God's Love. Yes, I was going through changes in my life, and maybe a few hardships, but I was not abandoned. I felt my sadness lift, replaced by a certainty that I would not take a single step alone. The Prophet, visible or not, would accompany me every step of the way, both at the school and off the mountain.

From the beginning Del, the Prophet, has inspired me to take the love and light that I experienced every time I set foot on the property and bring it with me into my daily life. Singing HU and appreciating the Hand of the Divine that touches my life on a daily basis has helped me draw nigh to God and deepen my awareness of that sacred, unbreakable connection. There is stability and love in my life now that I did not even dream of then.

That day God declared His Heavenly Love for me. The sky full of spiritual light was a Divine gift that brought a profound healing. Fears and doubts fell away, replaced by a confidence that I could experience the Prophet in all areas of my life and not just when I was at class. To walk in the Love of God is immensely personal and a direct reflection of one's relationship with the Divine. My relationship with the Prophet has grown over the last twenty years. It has enhanced all my other relationships and delivered me to the very abode of my Creator.

How grateful I am that God never abandons His children. He provides healing, clarity, protection, and a Prophet here in the physical to teach us, guide us, and walk with us all the way back to the Heart of God. Thank you Del, for guiding me on this sacred journey.

Written by Chris Comfort

52

He Came to Us

One of the greatest benefits for students of the Prophet is his ability to meet with them inwardly, regardless of their physical location. His ability to teach inwardly within the spiritual realms and the physical waking state is cause for exponential growth. In a very real sense the student is never alone, and spiritual growth can carry on continuously.

On August 2, 2015 there was a HU Sing on the mountain at the Nature Awareness School in Virginia. I inwardly asked my spiritual guide, the Prophet, Del Hall, if I could join them from where I physically live in the Hudson Valley of New York State. My friend had asked me if I would be attending the HU Sing and I relayed to her that I was going to joyfully sing from home. She asked if she could join me and I was thrilled by her request; I value HU and for her to value HU too opened my heart.

An hour before the HU sing was to begin we walked along Arden Trail to a point my friend loves that overlooks the Hudson River. We came upon an incredible vista of West Point to the left with the Hudson Highlands in the distance, and the shoreline of Garrison to the right. It was a beautiful view and it was a perfect day; no humidity in the air, sunny with the sky speckled with puffs of cumulus clouds. After we found our own niches to sit in upon the rock, we looked out feeling especially grateful as we watched and heard a gaggle of geese take flight from the water to the sky. It was a beautiful sight and I shared how my spiritual teacher Del likes geese and their sound, and how they mate for life. I said that I could not help but know that he was with us at that moment.

As we sat to take it all in, we noticed something floating out beyond on the water. I thought it looked like a package wrapped in a brown paper bag and my friend said it looked like a life preserver. It was too far to tell but either way I recognized how being able to sing HU was a gift to me and my lifeline as well. I then read out loud the Weekly Inspiration "Nourished in the Light of God," and then we sang HU for twenty minutes with about ten minutes of silence afterward. As we sang, the sounds around us increased. The cicada in the tree to our left sang along with us. Loudly I heard a goose singing too and I opened my eyes to view this one goose swimming close to us singing out its call as we sang out our prayer to God. In the distance, the gaggle of geese joined in. A train now passed by with the HU in its whistle, and the waves from boats that must have coasted by lapped upon the rocks, sounding like ocean waves. A gust of the perfect wind blew upon us. It was Heavenly.

As we sang, the Love of God was with us and I experienced this: spiritually and inwardly, the Prophet, Del Hall was on the water in a boat that looked similar to a canoe but very steady and sturdy. He paddled up to us and invited me in and I was able to step in without feeling off balance. We sat together enjoying the serene experience. Being in his presence immediately uplifted me and filled me with a love for God. As he paddled, we came upon the floating object on the water's surface. He encouraged me to reach over the side of the boat and grab it. I eagerly did. It was a package and was in fact wrapped in the paper of a brown bag! It was addressed to me, with my full name on it and with the word "Soul" in large letters. As I carefully opened it, savoring every moment of peeling the tape from the paper, I thought of my husband because that is how he opens his gifts; slowly and savoring the experience as the contents are revealed. When the package was loosened, a huge beam of light escaped right out, up, and from it. We were outside of God's beam of white, pure Light, and inside of it as well. My friend was there with us. She was on the rock singing HU and on the boat at the same time.

From this huge beam made of light and sound, a strand of light came out and went into my heart and I noticed that the Prophet had an individual beam coming from his heart which went directly into mine. I was filled with such love that is really indescribable. I was enveloped into It. The magnificence of this beam of God's Light covered our original view and beyond, and the space it took up was above and beyond our vision. I was in the midst of this beam of light that went from the river to well into the sky and beyond, and with this, we were still, calm, and at peace yet full of such intense joy and happiness and complete love.

In the beam I knew the sacred Holy Book lay. I was encouraged to open the book randomly and read from it. There at home, I knew I was to do this too, and I saw my husband and two boys immersed in God's loving Light. The Prophet and I stayed there and I gratefully and willingly accepted the love that was being offered. The goose then made its call again bringing me back into my body and the boom of the cannon from West Point made its point that we were in the protection of God's Love, inside of God's Heart, and in Its Light and Sound of eternity.

My friend expressed feeling at peace, calm and soothed. She said she would take it all with her and later on she let me know that she was still feeling it. I too have relived this experience every day since. Still sitting in the midst of love we saw what looked like a small white heart shaped piece of paper floating on the water coming toward us. My friend recognized this as a message that God surely loves her and we were very thankful for the love that we felt and received, and for the gift of singing HU, a prayer and love song to God.

As we stood to leave, a beautiful yellow tiger butterfly floated gently by reminding us that God's Love is all around and could transform us if we allowed it to do so. I knew I wanted to take that with me and share it. Later as we walked and talked and enjoyed the many different viewpoints that single goose flew by us, calling out to us letting us know it was near, as I have surely come to know in the depths of my heart that He truly is.

Written by Moira Cervone

53

The Precious Moment of Now

God's Light and Love flows spiritually through the Prophet into the world. It has always been this way - for all time. God never leaves us without someone authorized to pass on His Light. The names, faces, and scope of their individual missions change with the passing of the centuries, but at their core, God's eternal Light and Love continue to flow. Learning to become present in this presence is key to living an abundant life - here and now.

It was late summer in 2006 and I was attending a spiritual retreat at the Nature Awareness School. Del was about to take us on a journey into the inner worlds of Spirit. As a Prophet of God he is authorized and uniquely qualified to help Souls discover their true nature and learn about the nature of the Divine. He does this in part by providing opportunities to have direct personal experiences with Spirit, the Light and Sound of God. One quality I have come to appreciate and value is that of the present moment, because Soul lives in the present and because God gives us life one precious moment at a time. This is something the Prophet has taught me through experiences such as this one.

He began with a prayer that we would feel and know God's Love for us in some way. I was relaxed and looking forward to whatever was in store, grateful for this opportunity to continue to grow spiritually, something that is very important to me. We sang HU, a love song to God. It was totally dark with no physical light, but I could see a brightening as we sang. With my eyes opened or closed I saw that the room was getting lighter, and I could see the other students and the room around us.

I became aware of a beam or column of white light coming into the center of the room. It grew very bright. Del asked us to look down at our feet and take note of what we saw. Spiritually, my legs were out-stretched in front of me. I looked at them and noticed an old crude splint on my right leg and only a stump in place of my foot. It reminded me of a medical contraption one might see used in the 1800's or an earlier era such as this. The light intensified to a brilliant white, which became concentrated like a laser beam and zapped my right leg. The splint and stump were gone and I was no longer crippled or constrained by them. The splinted leg and stump symbolized some sort of impediment, passion of the mind, faulty thinking, or negative attitude I held that was holding me back spiritually. I trusted that since I was not shown specifically what it meant then it did not matter. Whatever it was had been removed by the Grace of God's Light and I was grateful for it.

I spiritually rose up and went with the Prophet. I no longer saw myself in physical body form, but as a ball of light, Soul, just as my Father in Heaven had created me long ago. I felt boundless and free! We flew and went into a kind of warp speed where I could see stars and light passing by incredibly fast. A burst of light came from the center of where we were traveling, then all became calm and still. I felt a sense of deep peace, love, and total trust. There was no time, no thought. I was immersed in the present moment and experienced an awesome now-ness for what seemed an eternity.

We began to sing HU once again as a group and the Prophet and I continued our journey. He brought me to one of the inner spiritual temples. Once inside, we went directly to the beam of light that was flowing into the center of the temple. I noticed it was the same beam that had entered the physical room we were in when we started and it was the same light that had healed me. As above so below. The Prophet walked over to It and stepped inside. When he did so, he became the beam of light. What I witnessed was that spiritually the Prophet was the beam, the light itself. He then brought me into It with him. Even though we were in our Soul bodies as light, I could see his eyes as if we were in the physical. I looked deep into them and saw an expansive nothingness and everything in them. Now was all that existed. I felt a joyful peace and contentment just being in this eternal moment with him.

Still inside the beam of light, I became aware of a shower of golden light raining down upon me. It was a strong windy kind of rain that cleansed me inside and out. I felt it scouring the spiritual dirt and impurities away and the wind blew me dry. I saw an image that looked like Niagara Falls and I jumped into it becoming immersed in the Holy Spirit and Its waters of life. It was beautiful, both cleansing and strengthening. It felt like a continuation of what had occurred earlier, nurturing the healing and replacing what had been removed with something positive. I continued looking into the Prophet's deep, endless, loving eyes at peace and totally in the moment. I felt so many things at once: peace, safety, security, perfection, stillness, love, and appreciation.

Overtime, with the Prophet's continued help, I have assimilated and integrated realizations, truth, and wisdom from sacred experiences like this one into my life. I spend a lot less time walking around in a daze of thoughts and emotions, thinking of past mistakes or worrying about the future. I am more at peace. When truly present, not merely physically there, I can listen better and be more sensitive to the needs of others. I am able to slow down and savor things in life like a beautiful sunrise, watching my kitty wake from sleep, enjoying a peaceful drive into work, or finding satisfaction in doing my best at whatever task or daily chore I am doing. Life is just sweeter. I have found the splendor of living is best experienced in the moment and that learning to be more fully present with the inner presence of the Prophet does truly lead one to a life more abundant.

Written by Lorraine Fortier

54

Journey to Tibet

If this beautifully written piece does not excite and inspire you with grand possibilities, then I do not know what will. Although this testimony is about going to a temple, which is covered more fully in section three, it fits better here. The experience was one that helped cleanse and condition the author rather than teaching the higher ways of God.

Fresh snow danced across the huge stone steps leading up to the doorway of an ancient Tibetan monastery. The jagged peaks of the Himalayan Mountains towered around us silhouetted by the fading evening light. Slowly, the temple door opened.

My body was thousands of miles away sitting peacefully in Virginia. Our spiritual journey was being guided by Del Hall. After singing HU, a love song to God, my consciousness had shifted naturally away from my body much like in a dream, to the distant Tibetan evening. Del's whole class waited excitedly on the stone steps. This is a very real place; our spiritual journey had brought us here in full consciousness.

An ancient monk clothed in white reverently greeted Del by the immense wooden doorway. They spoke for a moment and observed our group of newcomers. As the door opened it revealed a massive rotunda bursting with light. The light filled my being with hope, reverence, and love. This was no ordinary light. It was the Light of God. As the light shone upon our group I felt it purify, uplift, and nourish me spiritually. Clearly this was no ordinary temple. It was a true Temple of God, ordained and sustained by Him directly, unspoiled by the hand of man, and accessible to man only under the guidance of a true Prophet of God.

Del and the white-robed monk led us into the temple. Our small group paused just inside the door, absorbing the scene with awe. Workers in the temple moved purposefully about the rotunda busy in the responsibilities of this sacred sanctuary. The light seemed to come from everywhere at once, filling every corner and leaving no shadows. I watched the white-robed monk ascend a beautifully curved staircase, his hand upon an ornate golden banister.

He observed our group steadily. Slowly his gaze met mine and he spoke a single word: "Love." The energy in his voice entered my heart like an arrow! The single word spoke more than many volumes of literature, more than any eloquent speech. It was more than a syllable, more than a word. A mountain of wisdom and meaning surged behind it. It reached deep within me, speaking to the innermost part of my being, Soul, the true self.

The power of his message still reverberating within me, a gentle hand touched my arm. A worker from the temple led me to a hidden staircase descending into the foundation of the temple. He motioned me forward and I walked carefully down the stairs. Before me hung a narrow rope bridge leading to a stone platform. In the middle of the platform a small fire burned. And on the other side of the fire was the white-robed monk himself, sitting hooded and cross-legged. Behind him stood two full bookshelves holding ancient texts from forgotten kingdoms.

I crossed the bridge eagerly, but with a slow and measured pace. I sat across the fire from him and his deep gray eyes met mine. Immeasurable love and peace emanated from him. Not a word was spoken but I found myself drawn into his eyes, like an invisible force pulling me into another world. I traveled into his eyes as Soul. Everything changed; eternity seemed to exist in a moment. The temple guardian's endless eyes became my entire universe. Love was everywhere, but not love as I had known it before, it was a love that transcended emotion, time, religion, everything. I had truly experienced God's Love. In the days following this experience I was able to share it with the class. Others had similar experiences, personalized for their own spiritual growth. Del guided me in understanding these sacred events. He told me that this teacher had used a single word, such as "Love," to teach others before. Since the class the word he spoke has unfolded into hundreds of different nuances and applications.

Del explained that the basement seemed to represent the "cave of fire," a spiritual rite of passage that all seekers must go through on their journey home to God. This is a period of great trial and tribulation. This proved to be an accurate interpretation, for the next several years were a period of intense honesty and self-discovery. This was not always easy! But it led to a state of greater peace, freedom, and stability.

Somewhat, one might say, like crossing the narrow rope bridge in the temple onto the solid stone platform.

Although I had previously taken a wilderness skills class, this experience took place during my first spiritual retreat. In the ten years that have followed, it became clear that this was only the tip of the iceberg.

Written by David Hughes

55

My Key to God's Blessings

God's Light plays an integral part in purifying the seeker so that he may be able to accept more of God's Love and teachings. The Light of God removes barriers to lasting growth such as fear, vanity, anger, and unworthiness. Again the seeker was taken to a temple for the purpose of his growth, not so much the higher ways of God. Once the barriers are gone (or at least lessened - it's a process) God's truths and blessings are easier to accept and integrate into the seekers life. At this point one starts operating more as their true self, Soul, and life becomes an even greater joy to live.

I have been a student at the Nature Awareness School for over twenty years, with a desire for a more abundant life. I seek an ever-closer relationship with God, with a life filled with more love, peace, joy, and meaning. I seek to give more love to others as a husband, father, friend, and teacher. I seek to live life from the higher perspective as Soul, which was created to do these things. These are some of the aspects of the abundant life that God would like all His children to enjoy.

But there are stumbling blocks to receiving these blessings that only the presence of the Prophet can remove. There are limits to what I can do on my own. Along the way I have been shown that I've carried limiting burdens of fear, anger, and worry all my life. They were so familiar to me that they were hard to give up, even though they are a heavy load to shoulder. Over the years God's loving Grace, given through His Prophet Del Hall, has steadily freed me of more and more roadblocks to an abundant life. Only after these burdens began to lift, and I enjoyed the resulting sense of lightness and freedom, did I begin to grasp the magnitude and necessity of the Prophet's help. Only the Prophet is authorized by God to take us into the Heavens. This cleansing continues and there is more room in my heart to receive the abundance of God's blessings. What follows is one of many healing experiences in the Light and Sound of God that the Prophet has brought to me.

At a recent spiritual retreat at the Nature Awareness School, we sang HU, a love song to God. The group was led by Del Hall, God's

Prophet. In my heart was a prayer to draw nigh, closer to God. With my physical ears I could hear both the beautiful HU and the words of the Prophet. He offered us the opportunity to surrender our fear, anger, and worries. The love in his voice, the Prophet's voice, touched me deeply. That love opened my heart to consciously receive more of God's blessings. My attention shifted to my spiritual eyes and ears. My inner view screen was flooded with softly swirling, warm blue light, which coalesced into the face of the Prophet, Del Hall. I was drawn to his eyes, which conveyed a deep measure of God's Love that words cannot do justice. I felt the Prophet's joy as he offered the priceless gift of accepting my fear, anger, and worry. I gratefully surrendered these to him, happily giving them over. I felt a heavy burden lift, more than I knew I carried, bringing on a state of deep relaxation, peace, and comfort. With this new feeling of lightness came an awareness of moving through God's Heavens.

The Prophet had still more blessings in store for me. He took me through regions of purple and then golden white light. We arrived at one of God's Temples in the inner worlds. The temple itself was made of golden white light.

The Prophet gave my hand over to the guardian of this temple, who then led me into a beam of white light. Once I got inside the beam I found myself standing in a living cascade of God's Love, a pulsating waterfall of light. I cupped my hands together and drank double handfuls. The Prophet encouraged me to drink even more deeply of God's Light and Sound. I tilted my head back and gulped all that I could. God's Light and Sound washed through me, at once cleansing and nourishing and healing me from head to toe, both inside and out. At the same time I sensed an expansion of my heart, giving and receiving more of God's Love. From another perspective I saw that at the same time I was cradled in the arms of the Prophet. I was rocked gently back and forth. I was at once loved, cherished, protected, and secure. I could feel the power of God's Love in the Prophet's arms.

Who would want to leave those arms? I certainly did not. I only did so reluctantly when called back to my physical body. As I returned I was given still more gifts, blessings to take with me. I was given the certainty that I am always held in the Prophet's arms, where I am loved, protected, nurtured, and cherished. Another gift is that the Prophet takes me back to relive the experience, which continues to sustain me. A still further gift is that I have more love in my heart for the Prophet.

The Prophet has God's authority to safely carry us into the Heavens while we live in our physical bodies. There we are immersed in God's Light and Sound. As Soul we directly and purely experience the blessings of God's Love. With the Prophet's help the blessings of our Heavenly experiences are integrated into our daily lives. With his help we operate in our daily lives more as Soul, manifesting the best of what we were created to be. With his help I personally am a better husband, father, friend, and teacher. I do enjoy a bigger heart with a greater capacity to give and receive love. I am closer to God. I am blessed with an abundant life. The Prophet loves, protects, and guides me each step of the way.

Written by Irv Kempf

Section Three

Section Three

Traveling the Heavens

Now that proper preparation has occurred, usually over several years, the student is ready to travel with the Prophet safely into the vast spiritual worlds of God. In these higher worlds called planes, mansions, or Heavens the student is shown God's teachings and truth directly. By teaching through spiritual travel, certain spiritual understandings, concepts, and even the truest meaning of scripture is attainable. Over time students develop a rare view of life, of God and God's Love for them, of the representatives of God, and even of themselves as Soul. There is no better way to know God's teachings than to experience them yourself.

The testimonies in this section cover two important areas: traveling to God's Temples and traveling to the Abode of God. Students are guided by the Prophet and travel spiritually to temples of learning located in the various Heavens. These are Holy places where nothing but God's Living Truth can exist. The Light of God is extremely concentrated in each temple and comes directly from the Source. God assigns a primary teacher to each temple. One only gets to these sacred temples of learning by invitation and if they are escorted by the Prophet.

Also included in this section we share real experiences of Soul visiting the Abode of God. The Souls who persevered years of training and testing are now among those whom the Prophet guides home to God. They are now spiritual teachers in training and are used to guide and bless those who wish to learn God's ways and truth. They are now the sacred and trusted inner circle of God's Prophet and their duties are not taken lightly. They carry the inner Prophet with them, bringing Light to all who are receptive.

The primary message of this book is: God wants you to KNOW that you can truly have a more personal and loving relationship with the Divine. Your relationship with the Divine has the potential to be more profound, personal, and loving than any organized religion currently teaches on Earth. The Nature Awareness School is NOT a religion, it is a school. God and His Prophet are NOT disparaging of any religion of love. However, the more a path defines itself with its teachings, dogma, or tenets, the more "walls" it inadvertently creates between the seeker and God. Sometimes it even puts God into a smaller box. God does not fit in any box. The Prophet is for all Souls and is purposely not officially aligned with any path, but shows respect to all.

Part of my mission is to share more of what is spiritually possible for you as a child of God. Few Souls know or understand that God's Prophet can safely guide God's children to their Heavenly home while they are still alive physically. Taking a child of God into the Heavens is not the job of clergy. Clergy has a responsibility to pass on the teachings of their religion exactly as they were taught, not to add additional concepts or possibilities. If every clergy member taught their own personal belief system no religion could survive for long. Then the beautiful teachings of an earlier Prophet of God would be lost. Clergy can be creative in finding interesting and uplifting ways to share their teachings, but their job is to keep their religion intact. However, God sends His Prophets to build on the teachings of His past Prophets, to share God's Light, and to guide Souls to their Heavenly home.

There is ALWAYS MORE when it comes to God's teachings and truth. No one Prophet can teach ALL of God's ways. It may be that the audience of a particular time in history cannot absorb more wisdom. It could be due to a Prophet's limited time to teach and limited time in a physical body on Earth. Ultimately, there is ALWAYS MORE! Each of God's Prophets bring additional teachings and possibilities in ways to draw closer to God, building on the work and teachings of former Prophets. That is one reason why Prophets of the past ask God to send another; to comfort, teach, and continue to help God's children grow into greater abundance. Former Prophets continue to have great love for God's children and want to see them continue to grow in accepting more of God's Love. One never needs to stop loving or accepting help from a past Prophet in order to grow with the help of the current Prophet. All true Prophets of God work together and help one another do God's work.

56

My Journey to a Temple Of God

Within the Heavenly worlds are spiritual temples. In essence they are "God's churches." These are very real places where the truth of God is kept pure, away from the polluting minds of men. The Prophet is a spiritual guide qualified to help you journey to these temples to gain in love and wisdom.

During a recent class Del, the Prophet, blessed our group by spiritually taking us to visit one of God's Temples in the inner worlds. These are not physical places, but are more real than any brick and mortar building. We sang HU, a love song to God, and then Del guided us on this journey to the inner worlds.

I arrived on the temple's porch to see the door held open by the temple guardian and a beautiful light pouring out. When I stepped inside, the light was so bright that it was all I could see. My eyes hurt physically at times it was so bright. This was the Light of God. I do not have words to fully describe what I experienced. I know that everything I could ever need is within that Light. I could describe it as love, peace, security, or comfort and it was all those qualities but the words seem to diminish it; it was so much more. I know it supported me, nourished me, filled every lack, and reassured every insecurity. It did all of these things and more, but in the moment I was aware solely of the presence of the Voice of God and felt only reverence and humility. This was nothing I could have earned, but was given this gift by the Grace of God.

I am forever changed by this light. Even the sunlight the next morning was different though it was not the sun that warmed my heart. I closed my eyes and found myself immersed in the Light of God. A moment in eternity lasts forever. I will always carry this precious experience in my heart. I am very loved.

Written By Jean Enzbrenner

57

God's Sound Took Me Home

The "Voice of God" or the "Holy Ghost" is singular, but it manifests as spiritual light and spiritual sound. Conscious experience with these aspects of Spirit is critical for those seeking to more fully know the ways of God. Not only do they contain everything Soul needs, they help Soul on Its journey. For it is the mighty sound current that Soul follows home to God.

During a weekend retreat a group of us sat with Del and did a spiritual exercise. Del, the Prophet, has the authority to speak the Word of God, to teach, and to bless Souls with sacred experiences of Divine Love. This extends to his ability to take Souls/us to God's Heavens. That night I was blessed with a gift of God's Love and a visit home to God.

During this experience we sang HU, a beautiful love song to God. This night our HU seemed especially sweet and beautiful and filled with love. With my physical eyes closed I felt our HU go out to God. Within seconds they returned back to us in the form of a wave of Divine Love. We continued to HU and each HU returned to us more beautiful than the ones before it. God's Love washed over and through me, cleansing me, and nourishing me. In that moment I lacked nothing. I had no needs, no wants. Everything was perfect. I was so full of love and gratitude.

Then came an incredible resonating quality deep within our HU, an indescribable sound. This sound, this vibration, washed through every part of me and my being! Then by the Grace of God, the Prophet took me home to God on the spiritual sound wave. I felt this sound draw me, guide me, and carry me back home towards God. It felt like it bent, folded, or collapsed everything I would call time and space, in on itself, until it was in one place. This "place" was more beautiful than anything I could have ever imagined. Time ceased to exist and I had no idea if it was a second or hour, but for a brief moment in eternity, I was literally back home, inside the Heart of God.

There was an ancient familiarity, a sense of completeness, a beauty, a peace, a joy, a love, and mercy beyond what I could comprehend or describe. It was pure love. I was held like a child within "a peace that surpasses all understanding." There is really no way to put words to it. Being able to bring a little bit of this back into my daily life is such a blessing. I feel I have been graced with a small glimpse of the "peace" and "the more abundant life" that is offered in the Bible.

Several religions know about the Light of God but few know about the Sound of God. The Sound is one half of the Holy Spirit and the Light is the other half. This spiritual sound carried me back to the Heart of God. Del is fluent in the "Language of the Divine," the Word, the Light and Sound of God. He can show us the way and guide us on our journey back home, to the love and peace we all seek, deep within our hearts.

Written by Jason Levinson

58

Divine Wisdom Written Upon an Ink-less Page

This wonderfully written account of journeying spiritually to a temple within the Heavenly realms contains many pearls of wisdom. Among them, God has given us free will to follow our heart and sculpt a life that brings love and beauty into the world. Through His Prophet, God is there at every step of the way to guide and comfort us. Ultimately though we must walk the path for ourselves - this includes living our life.

One evening during a retreat at the Nature Awareness School, after singing HU for some time, I was taken on an inner journey to a temple where my prayers and questions were answered in a most unexpected way. Although my physical eyes were closed as my body sat in the mountains of Virginia, I became aware that inwardly, I was being welcomed into a Temple of God, a place where Divine wisdom was available in vast quantities. A Prophet of God welcomed me to this temple. I knew that I had come there by invitation, and my journey was made possible by the Prophet, and the Grace of God.

In this temple I was aware of deep maroon tapestries on the walls, and rich curtains which separated areas for private prayer and contemplation from a main hall, a great rotunda. As I looked around the rotunda, I could not miss the golden book enshrined in a great beam of white and golden light passing through the center of the room. The book seemed almost alive, glowing with the Love and wisdom of God. I had experienced other temples before, and to me this temple felt much the same as others, which I had been privileged to experience.

These different temples, though staffed by different teachers and built in different styles reflecting the tastes of different cultures and ages all had one thing in common – the living, flowing Love and wisdom of God. Unlike the houses of worship found in the cities and hamlets of humanity, which each reflect a different view of what we think God might wish to teach, these inner temples are filled with the living waters of Divine Love and wisdom, actively flowing direct from their Source, unfiltered by human shortcomings.

At this time, in this particular temple, I noticed the floors and walls, which seemed to be a polished white marble. I moved across this great floor to the book, and reached into the beam glowing with light, and humming with Divine Sound. As I made contact with the book, which really seemed to be an aspect of this beam of light and love itself, I found myself drawn into what seemed to be another dimension, greater and more beautiful than the great temple itself. Surrounded by love and deep peace beyond understanding, I was aware that I was not separate from this love and peace, but actually a part of it. Accepting more of my identity as a true child of God, I became more aware that what I experienced is actually a part of my true nature, not simply as a man, but as Soul.

After some time, perhaps a minute or two that seemed to stretch out across a beautiful eternity, I gently came back into the main part of the temple. Then, just as gently, my consciousness shifted away from this experience and back into the woods of Virginia. As I opened my eyes I brought back not only the deep peace and love of this experience, but also an actual page number to look up in a physical book of scripture. Excited to see what other wisdom might await me in this book, I opened to the page I was given on the inner, and found one of the very few pages in the entire book, which are completely blank!

In prayer as I sought to better understand this experience and incorporate it into my life, I saw that the blank white page rhymed with the polished white marble of the temple floor and walls. As I discussed the experience with my teacher, he helped me realize that this was actually a very direct answer to a prayer I often had at that time in my life. I had been asking for God to show me what God wants me to do in life, and what my next steps should be on my journey in service to the Divine. It became clear that the choice is actually mine, as it always has been. God has given us each free will to live life on our own terms, and use our gifts as we see fit. Divine suggestions and guidance are available, but our course in life is mainly up to us. Free will is a reality only if we use it, and actively choose our destiny in harmony with the Divine. As we boldly begin to create the life we wish to live, the Light of God helps us see the best choices more clearly.

The weakest part of the human consciousness wishes to be told what to do. It takes strength and courage to set a course into the unknown, seeking help from God every step of the way. The meek shall inherit the earth, but the bold and courageous may inherit the Kingdom of Heaven. And so it was that God wrote an answer to my prayer and questions upon a page with no ink, presented to me in a sacred temple where fresh wisdom flows out like the cool, refreshing waters of a spring. When next you pray, why not ask God to have the Prophet bring you too to such a place? There is room for you, and there is a Prophet who is ready to take you for a visit. What would you like to do?

Written By Timothy Donley

59

Nourished in the Light of God

Tuning in with Spirit during prayer is one of the best ways for you, Soul, to receive nourishment. One of the purest prayers is singing HU, an ancient name for God, as an expression of love and gratitude to God. Singing HU alone is wonderful, but there is truly something glorious about joining with a multitude to do so. The following is an experience from one of the group HU sings we hosted on the mountain.

While attending a HU Sing at the Nature Awareness School, I had an experience in the Light and Sound of God, which is a more definitive name for the Holy Spirit or Voice of God. I have been a student there since 2005. In this time I have seen this Light many times and heard the Sound in various ways. I know that it is only by the Grace of God that I am able to have these experiences. Each experience builds on the next, and I realize these precious gifts are not random. There is a very personal nature to my experiences and how love is expressed to me.

As Del led us in the HU song, I listened to his voice and the voice of many Souls expressing their love and gratitude to God. I began to perceive a growing ball of blue light at my inner vision (third eye or spiritual eye). The blue turned to intense white light, and I had a sense of floating, as if weightless. My teacher was with me, as the inner guide now, and we began to rise up inside of this light. Before long I was bobbing as if I was on a raft in an ocean. The nourishment of this light came in waves. In the light, I experienced wisdom, peace, love, joy, and boundlessness. I was a part of a living sea of God's Light and Sound. I was cleansed, cared for, and uplifted in this presence.

There was texture to this Light and Sound. It was not static, but alive. It came from a living God and I became more alive in this experience. I know more of my true nature and some of the nature of God as a result. A deep realization spoke to my heart and I knew it as the Voice of God. "I love you - I love all my children - You are a part of my living essence."

These words opened me even more to love and I prayed never to take this experience for granted, any of my experiences. Part of me knows that language and words cannot truly convey my experience and how it continues to deepen my realization of God and of my true self. I am transformed by the solid foundation of knowing, not believing that a living, loving, and merciful presence does exist and that we exist because of the endless love it pours out. This continues to inspire me to discover and rediscover my Divine gifts and live them out loud. That is why I share this.

My story is not about how loved I am, but how loved we all are. We are never alone. There was a time in my life when I felt alone. I did not know or perceive this Light and Sound, this loving presence. I only discovered it by the Grace of God leading me to the Prophet, and the tools and truth I have since learned at the Nature Awareness School. This has made it possible for me to know that God is real. It's Light and Sound nourishes, animates, and sustains all creation.

My heart tells me that God wants to feed all of us, but we must open our "spiritual mouths" to accept this nourishment. Singing HU is one way that is available to all, regardless of our spiritual path or where we are in our relationship with God.

Written by Tash Canine

60

Child of God – Really

You are so much more than your temporal physical body. You are Soul, an eternal child of God, created out of the Light of God. Many find this hard to believe but nonetheless, it is true. Beneath our shortcomings as humans, we are spiritually perfect. The more you allow the Prophet to let you experience, know, and identify with your true self, Soul, the more the "earthly baggage" will lose its grip.

We gathered in the Beach House at the Nature Awareness School, ready to sing HU. Del explained the HU and then said that you might know intellectually that you are a child of God, but not fully understand what exactly that means, how sacred, and special that really is. In time and with spiritual experience you may gain true understanding. I thought I knew what it meant to be a child of God, but wondered if I was about to learn more.

During the quiet time after singing HU, I flew rapidly through a narrow dim tunnel and came out at God's Ocean. I recognized this as the twelfth Heaven, one of the very high Heavenly worlds. I was distinctly aware that I was Soul. Instead of a body, I was my true self, a ball of light. I sparkled with pure rays of white light. Within my light was nothing dark or negative. I knew intuitively that it would be impossible for anything negative to stick to Soul.

When I had exited the tunnel, I escaped the bodies that cover Soul and disguise the perfection of God's creation. The disguise is so good that it even fools us. Anger, fear, worry, and their relations are not Soul. We are not our defilements or our mistakes. We are children of God, perfectly created with virtually limitless potential. As I looked out at the water I recognized sparkles in it made of the same light as me. God created Soul out of Itself, in Its image, Its own light. Yet I also recognized that God is much more than Soul could ever be, even if Soul's potential was fully realized.

I was not alone. The Prophet brought me there and remained beside me. As a ball of light he embraced me, His Light enveloping mine. Within him, I felt closer to God, with all that God knows and sees at the Prophet's fingertips. I cannot find my way home alone. I need a guide, the Prophet, to show me the way.

As I opened my eyes following the HU, the world looked different. I knew deeper than before that I am Soul, a child of God. Beneath my human coverings is Soul, my true self and yours. We are both, you and I, one of God's glorious creations. Sing HU, look within, and ask the Prophet to show you your true self. A grand adventure awaits!

Written by Jean Enzbrenner

61

Into the Heart of God

I sometimes wonder what it would be like to read experiences, of the magnitude contained within this book, for the first time. They are beyond profound. Will you be able to accept the truth they contain? Will you be able to accept the reality of conscious travel into the Heavenly worlds to visit with an aspect of God Himself? I hope so. I hope you are inspired and excited by the very real possibility these true stories contain.

Over the winter Nature Awareness School students are invited to attend small group weekend retreats. The focus is on strengthening our relationship with the Divine and further developing our spiritual survival skills necessary for the journey home to God. One of Del's gifts as the Prophet is the ability to take Souls on inner travels into the vast Heavens. The experiences and blessings received during these visits can have lasting impact if a person's heart is open to accepting them and keeps them alive through remembrance.

We began to sing HU, a love song to God. The Prophet brought me to the beach of a vast spiritual ocean within the Heavenly worlds. It was not a typical ocean as seen in the physical world. The sand and water here were alive with the Love of God. The sacredness and reverence I experienced brought me to my knees. I was in the Presence of God and I burned with a desire to serve and give everything to It. Love was going back and forth between me and this Divine Presence. I was caught up inside a great vortex that brought me out into the water. I began to swim relaxed and steadily in this ocean of love. I felt the gentle rise and fall of the swells. My breaths now in sync with Its rhythm. The swells became like breaths taken by lungs within the ocean. I was aware of being inside what seemed like a huge rib cage, feeling its diaphragm rising and falling in rhythm with the ocean swells.

The Prophet then brought me into a large hand that came up out of the water. I was in the Hand of God. In it I felt comfort and love and was safe and secure. The hand brought us up into Its Heart where showers of Divine Spirit's

Light and Sound poured down on me. It was intense enough that it physically pinned me back to the sofa. Suddenly I felt like I was on a rocket that had blasted off and rose up high coming to rest in a place of great love. I viewed various outer scenes from within this beautiful place. Everything I saw had a whitish blue hue to it. I was shown lands in turmoil with violence and battles but I was not endangered or impacted by it. I was at peace, safe in this place of great love in the Heart of God. What I experienced was but one aspect of God's infinite reality and it was magnificent! I did not want to leave but I knew a part of me would always be there.

In a previous inner experience with the Prophet I was being taught how to travel in the Soul body with him. In this experience he showed me I had the freedom to move about in the inner worlds by focusing my attention wherever I wanted to go. I could essentially "travel" by gently shifting my focus. This is not physical travel but spiritual travel, or a change in one's state of awareness or consciousness. I remembered his teaching me this skill so I put it to use to go back to the Heart of God with the Prophet and relive that experience.

Whenever I do this it is like taking a deep breath of Divine Spirit. It brings peace and relaxes me. I am quickly in a different frame of mind and have a broader and higher view of the situation and my surroundings. I am again able to feel the immense love within God's Ocean I was taken to visit. This is one way I draw nigh to God, by keeping the sacred experiences He blesses me with alive, and by allowing them to continue to nourish me.

Written by Lorraine Fortier

62

House of Liberation

When one comes to fully know that God loves them, through direct personal experience, it brings a deep and everlasting peace. With this peace comes clarity, which is such a blessing because life is full of difficult decisions.

Several years ago I was given an out-of-body experience where I was taken to a spiritual temple and given a wonderful gift. Ever since, it has blessed me in many very practical ways. The experience happened at a retreat at the Nature Awareness School. Our teacher was Del Hall, a true Prophet of God. It was during a time when I knew that my elderly mother, who had dementia, needed to be moved to a different place to live and I was seeking clarity on what would be best for all involved. Thoughts of how such a move would change her life and the lives of our family had been weighing heavily on me. I left those worries outside as I reverently entered the room.

As I sat with eyes closed in a group of other students, I thought of how grateful I am to be right here in this holy place at this particular time in my life. This gratitude put a smile on my face and opened my heart, helping me to be receptive to whatever God might communicate. We began to reverently sing HU, a love song to God. The sound was so beautiful! I focused on singing my love to God as purely as I could, not asking for anything. Within a few minutes, I felt myself being lifted up. My body was still sitting there, but as Soul, I was free of the body. I felt no fear or discomfort, knowing I was protected and guided by the inner spiritual teacher, the Prophet. He took me to a beautiful temple. We were greeted and welcomed by a refined, bearded being, who was the guardian of this temple, known as the House of Liberation.

As we reverently entered, I saw a brilliant golden and white light beam shining down from above onto an open book on a pedestal. The beam was wide enough for me to step into as I approached the book, the living Word of God, and looked at the open pages. There, clearly written in large letters were the words, "I LOVE YOU." There within the beam, I felt more loved than I had ever felt before, and a deep, deep inner peace and calm that I cannot describe with words. All the tension melted away in my gut and my entire being was freed from all worry about anything. This is truly the peace that Jesus spoke of, that surpasses all understanding.

The guardian then spoke to me these words; "This deep peace and love you are now experiencing, is yours at all times and everywhere you go, NO MATTER WHAT." The message permeated deeply into every part of me. This was a promise I could stake my life upon.

With that inner peace came clarity. My questions about moving my mother were immediately answered, and there was no uncertainty about it at all. I could see the benefits to her and all involved. Over the years since that profound experience, I continue learning to live more and more fully in that promise, aspiring to live every moment of every day in the clarity that comes with God's gift of deep inner peace and love. Whenever I catch myself stressing over something, whether it be a decision or a daunting task, I remember that promise, and immediately the stress melts away, a smile returns, and in that moment, I can make better decisions and lovingly do whatever needs to be done in that situation. What a glorious gift that keeps on giving, just when I need it! Thank you Prophet!

Written by Paul H. Sandman

63

Opportunity of a Lifetime

Many are content to squabble for scraps of God's Love and teachings. Others are soaring free from the bounds of Earth to the very Abode of God Himself to receive the ultimate spiritual nourishment. There is no judgment here - it is what it is. In God's perfect plan, and at the perfect time, everyone will eventually wake up and begin to yearn for more. They will begin craving to know more of God's truths and ways and look for a guide to lead them Home. If your good fortune has brought you to the Prophet - step through the door before it closes.

In the fall of 2008 I moved to Virginia from Michigan. I moved to Virginia because I wanted to be closer to the Nature Awareness School. It is here that I experienced God's Love and now realize that It has always been with me. I learned about my Divine nature as Soul. I learned about the sacred prayer, HU, and spiritual truths that have begun to slowly set me free of passions of the mind like anger and fear. Most important it was here I met Del, my spiritual guide, which has changed the course of my life.

I had recently been accepted to graduate school, but going there would mean I would not be as free to attend spiritual retreats at the Nature Awareness School. I had a dream, given to me by God, which helped me make the decision to move by showing me what was in my heart. In the dream I was asleep and was invited down to the school, but I took a detour and by the time I got there Del was gone. I was very upset that I had missed him. When I woke up I had a knowingness that gradually turned into a conviction that I needed to move closer. I did not want to miss out on the teachings or being with Del. There are windows of opportunity in life and this was mine. Del is the Prophet of our times, which means he can show the way home to the very Heart of God. It is a privilege to know him and be in his presence. I thank God that I was woken up spiritually allowing me to become a student and build a relationship with the Prophet.

In the summer of 2008 I was blessed to attend my first Reunion. This is an eight-day retreat in the mountains. It is a special week to focus on God and His Divine teachings of Light and Love.

I was given an experience during the retreat that I will never forget. The line from Amazing Grace, "I once was lost, but now I am found," means more to me now than ever. I was taken in full consciousness by the Prophet to the twelfth Heaven. This is sometimes called the Abode of God. I knelt in the sand on the edge of the ocean. I was told I could look up to see an aspect of God. Golden light, which was actually God loving me directly, blazed as I looked out across the dazzling water. Just then an eagle soared overhead. It swooped down and snagged a fish from the water. The majestic bird launched back in the air with the fish clutched in its talons. Then I became the eagle biting and tearing at the fish with excitement! Oh the joy to be able to fly! I felt the strength of the eagle and the freedom to be able to glide through the sky. At God's Ocean there is the absolute best spiritual nourishment to be found and consumed. God's Love nourished me like a fresh fish nourishing an eagle. I felt like a spiritual eagle soaring!

Before I met the Prophet I was in some ways like that fish, one of many Souls swimming in unison through life. Then the Prophet came and pulled me from my place and set my feet back upon the path of light and love. I was absorbed into the body of the Holy Spirit and made new by the Grace of God. Once I experienced Divine Love and myself as Soul there was no way I could go back to the old ways of life and be content. The fish is also a symbol of spiritual nourishment, which I found at the school. I was craving spiritual food and I still need it to thrive. It is as necessary as breathing.

As the eagle I was allowed to experience some of the attributes that God gives Soul: joy, strength, and freedom! We each have these and more God-given qualities, but swimming in our regular schools of life we are not often taught about the truth of Soul. I thank the Prophet for allowing me to become his spiritual student in this lifetime. I have learned what no earthly school could ever teach. I have been to Heaven! I have experienced God's Love and His Light and Sound! I know that I am Soul and so are my loved ones and friends! I also know that God loves you just as dearly. Are you like an eagle, just waiting to stretch your wings?

Written by Carmen Snodgrass

64

The Lord's Temple

Within the spiritual realms exist temples filled with the Light and Love of God. They are every bit, if not more, real than places you may visit here in the physical. They are "God's churches" where Soul may be taken to experience God's pure truth, unadulterated by man. In the following story the author experiences one of the core truths taught at the school. You are more than your physical self - you are Soul, a beautiful child of God.

One weekend last fall I was attending a three day spiritual retreat at the Nature Awareness School in the mountains of Virginia. The air was crisp and cool as the day rolled into evening. Outside the golden orange and red tree leaves danced in the wind. I felt sweet anticipation as my teacher Del, a true Prophet of God, began to lead us in a contemplation. While he spoke initially, all was now quiet in the room, as each of us journeyed inward.

The Prophet stands beside me in my inner vision. As Soul we approach the edge of a pond and I begin to see what is really before me. A temple arises out of the water. It is eternal; there is no end to this immense and beautiful temple, which forms. It is not like any building here in the physical. This building is alive, containing living truth, living water, and living love. It is a temple made out of love. God's Love.

Following inner prompting, I knew to look at my heart. I see myself as I truly am, without any shell. I see *Soul*. I, like you, am a very bright and beautiful light. This light is so bright it is almost blinding. As I look at myself and then again look up at God's Temple, I recognize that I am made of the same substance I see before me - *Love*.

With a grateful heart, I approach this temple by grace. I could not come here alone, it is only with the Prophet of God that one can enter these holy temples on the inner, and only with a grateful and loving heart. At the entrance stands the guardian welcoming me and everyone in our class with so much love. I feel incredibly blessed and come to tears of joy at this sacred opportunity.

As I walk inside this living temple the beauty is beyond words. To say I am standing on love may seem impossible, but I am. Everything is emanating bright light. Del IV's masterpieces of art surround the room. Some of his art adorns the classrooms at the physical Nature Awareness School. Yet unlike his paintings on Earth, these ones are actually alive, pulsating with the Light and Sound of God. Colors swirling and blending and dancing on the walls - art at its finest. Words cannot give true credit to their beauty. In the center of the room I see a beam of light and sound, which flows forth onto the floor.

I step inside and am given the opportunity to see this beam from a new direction, a new perspective. I look downwards. It is like a flower with a concentrated treasure of the most brilliant blue in the center. Life flows up and outward from this core. Like flowing water, the energy and love flowing forth emerge from this center. I am brought to tears of gratitude as this light flows into and through me. The blessing of being able to consciously travel here with the Prophet, and to then have my own personal, intimate experience with this beam of love is one that continues to touch my heart today. God is alive and showers His blessings upon us. By grace, I was given the eyes to see.

I become aware again of the Prophet, who has been beside me on this entire journey. Now he and I begin to dance, a dance of Soul. I experience freedom and joy with a depth that comes from being this close to the Divine. Slowly the experience comes to a close. I am escorted out of the temple and express gratitude to the Prophet. With awareness I return to my physical body. When I open my eyes in the classroom, I see the world differently. As Soul our true nature is to see the beauty and magnificence of God's creation with awe, wonder, and gratitude. As the art in the temple was alive and uplifting, so too are we. We are beautiful Souls with a majesty that only God can create. It has just been hidden and disguised beneath our skin. You are more than just your physical body.

There is more to me than my body. I am Soul! I am beautiful! Years ago these were just words to me. But after years of personal experiences with the Divine, thanks to my teacher Del, now I see the Divinity within me. It has been revealed by the Grace of God. Would you like to see clearer and witness the truth of who you really are? Would you like to travel to the Lord's Temples? Perhaps the Prophet can guide you too. Perhaps he can help you see who you truly are - *a beautiful Soul.*

Written by Molly Comfort

65

In Our Father's Eyes

This is an amazing testimony on visiting the abode of God. Traveling spiritually in full consciousness to the source of all - to the home of Our Father. Guided there by the Prophet to receive healing, revelation, comfort, and a profound insight - we are each loved unconditionally by God. Being able to accept this love changes everything.

Do you know that we are welcome in Heaven? Do you know that God loves you no matter what you are facing in life? Out of the many, many blessings that being a student of Del's has given me, this following experience stands out as the one that gave me an understanding that God's Love for us truly has no conditions. Knowing this has given me a peace that has changed how I walk through life.

Some years ago, I was going through a time where I was struggling with jealousy and envy. I was not comfortable in my own skin, and thought that if I was more like someone else or had what they had in their lives, then I would be happy. While logically I knew that this was unhealthy, I could not seem to shake it. In my eyes, I was not deserving of love.

During a week long spiritual retreat at the Nature Awareness School Del led us in singing HU. After some time, I became aware that I was in front of a huge ocean made entirely of God's Love. Instinctively, I knelt. I was not alone. Beside me were Souls as far as I could see. Each one of us was made of glowing, shimmering light. Each one of us was beautiful. We were each kneeling along this beach in love and reverence to Our Heavenly Father. As I looked out over the wide expanse, I saw pure white light reflecting in the distant water. The light came closer to me and I saw a form appear sitting in a gigantic chair. The Heavenly Father was seated before us. I could see and feel our love going out to Him with each HU, and then returning back to us in a beautiful rhythm.

As I was kneeling before this immense ocean of God's Love, I was experiencing such a deep, deep peace. I have never experienced this much peace in my life. I needed nothing and I lacked nothing. Peace filled every fiber of my being.

Tears streamed down my face, as I accepted the love that was being offered to me. Then, Our Heavenly Father arose and came towards me across the water. With such a gentleness, He lifted my head and kissed my forehead. "I love you and I am glad you are here." His eyes filled the sky, immense and loving. His Love continued to pour into me, filling every part of me.

I knew then, as I do now, that He loves me without conditions. He has the same love for you, no matter what you are struggling with inside or going through in life. Our Father truly loves us unconditionally, and accepting this love truly changes us.

For days, and now years later, I close my eyes and return to this living experience of God's Love. Seeing the love in my Heavenly Father's eyes, face to face, gave me a confidence in His Love for me that is unshakable. Thank you Del, the Prophet, for guiding me home to Heaven to meet Our Father, face to face.

Written by Molly Comfort

66

Gifts of Freedom

"How much pain they have cost us, the evils which have never happened." Thomas Jefferson

One Saturday evening at a three day Spiritual Retreat, we sang a long HU gently tapering off as Del said, "Thank you." The HU and discussion throughout the day had blessed all of us, but there was still more. We were invited to visit one of God's Temples in the inner worlds. Del, the Prophet began guiding us, both inwardly and outwardly. I took the Prophet's hands, turned as he did, and we were at the House of Liberation.

We walked up the steps onto the temple porch where I fell to my knees in reverence to be at a Temple of God. I have visited these temples many times and recognize more now, what a privilege it is to be there. Inside, the temple guardian greeted us and spoke about spiritual liberation. He said that it does not happen overnight, but over time and by degrees. Every HU, every moment listening to the Divine, can bring a degree of spiritual freedom. Over time, seemingly small things add up and may lead to a life changing realization. It seems that the single event changed everything and it did, but not without all the small moments that came before it. It is like years of freezing and thawing slowly expanding a crack until a rock suddenly breaks free and falls from the cliff. It seems to happen in a moment, but was years in the making.

Leaving the temple guardian, the Prophet led me to the heart of the temple where a book lay open on a pedestal. This book is the living Word of God, always fresh and perfect for the seeker in that moment. I read in golden script, "Live joyously," and then, as the Prophet urged me, I turned the page and read, "for I am with you." I have often hesitated to embrace life fearing all that could go wrong, all the mistakes I could make. These words reminded me that I am never alone; the Prophet is with me and loves me. Even if things appear to go wrong, all the love, support, and help I could ever need are right there. The Prophet's presence frees me to live with joy.

I turned and hugged the Prophet. He became a beam of the Light and Sound of God and I was within It. The light shimmered and flowed around me and through me. I leaned my head back and drank the light, watching it clean out any impurity I no longer needed. This precision healing cleans out negative things like fear or worry that I no longer need but leaves any still needed to learn and grow. I asked for it to wash away any resistance to truth. I drank more and the light broke black crust off my heart and washed it off me. I stayed as long as I could, wanting to be as clean as possible.

The only way to freedom is through the truth. Sometimes it seems that facing the truth would be uncomfortable or something I do not want to know. Resisting truth causes pain and discomfort, not the truth itself. Hidden in the dark, it grows until it seems enormous, impossible to solve. Often, simply admitting the truth to the Prophet and myself evaporates the problem. Only by accepting truth do I begin to see a solution.

I returned to my body full of love and blessings to bring greater freedom into my life. The experience was beautiful, but unless I remember it and integrate what I learned into my life, nothing changes. Freedom comes when I do my part. I received precious gifts, but they can only bring freedom if I remember them in my everyday life. That is my privilege and responsibility and that, too, is a gift from God.

Written by Jean Enzbrenner

67

"My Peace I Leave With You"

There is a deep, eternal peace available for you. Not world peace or the kind of peace from a joyful day of boating, but rather - a lasting peace of the heart. The peace that comes with seeing clearly, truly knowing the ways of God, and accepting His Love. With this peace, Soul comes into harmony with itself and the Divine, and man can rise above the trials and tribulations of life in the physical. This peace is your birthright as Soul and only need be awakened by drawing nigh to God and God's Prophet.

The Lord said to me, "My peace I leave with you," during a recent experience I had at Nature Awareness School. I had also read it in the Bible that Jesus once said this to his disciples. So I asked myself: what did that really mean? I do not presume to know completely, but I can tell you that there is a peace, which surpasses all understanding - something else I had read in the

Bible. I know this because the Prophet took me to the twelfth Heaven where I experienced these things myself. Peace was all there was and more.

It was a Sunday morning during one of the smaller classes held during the winter. Del invited us to join him in singing HU. As we sang I noticed his presence as the inner guide with me. Each HU became a wave of light and sound that we surfed in Soul bodies. With each wave the Prophet and I drew closer to a beach. Throughout this experience I heard various sounds. First the sound of wind, then a high pitched humming sound, which gave way to something like that of the sound of a whirlpool. We were on the returning sound wave; part of the Light and Sound of God that Soul must be linked with in order to go home to God.

We arrived at what appeared to be a beach of a great ocean. I felt a humble submission take over my whole being. I had to kneel. The Prophet knelt with me for a moment and then grasped my hand to lift me up. As I looked out from where we were an expansive horizon of blinding bright light was all there was. Emanating from this vista was a peace that is beyond anything I had ever felt. I was shown that some of God's peace was being distributed throughout the worlds during our HU song. I could see that the HU truly is a prayer that blesses many Souls I may never know.

The peace I experienced that morning is still with me today. Accepting the hand of the current Prophet of God leads to peace, security, and more. My ever-growing awareness and love for the Divine allows me to access this gift of God. It lives in my heart. I wondered if Jesus said those words so many years ago as an invitation to accept him and have this deep peace. I have come to realize that our Heavenly Father loves us very much. He always has a living Prophet to guide us home and distribute his blessings. He has given us a Comforter today. We do not have to wait. I am so grateful.

Written by Tash Canine

68

"I Love You"

It is one thing to be told, "God loves you." It is quite another if you are blessed to actually experience God's Love for yourself. The following testimony takes it even farther with the author being told from an aspect of God Himself that she was loved. To truly know deep down that God loves you is a rock to build your life on.

If you could travel to visit God and could hear God tell you directly "I love you," would it change you? It changed me when I was blessed with this sacred experience. One of the primary missions of the Prophet of God is to take you home to the Abode of God. While I was singing HU, a love song to God, during a retreat at the Nature Awareness School, the Prophet took me to an expansive and magnificent ocean where I was blessed to witness an aspect of God.

The Prophet and I were standing on the beach at the water's edge when I saw an enormous sphere of electric light over the ocean. I knew with every fiber of my being that I was witnessing an aspect of God; it was alive, active, and full of love. It was so magnificent and yet this was only a fraction of what God is. I was continuing to sing HU when I realized I was singing directly to God. I was being allowed, by the Divine, to express my deep love and reverence to God. Then something sacred and fortifying happened; I heard very loudly and clearly, with my physical ears, the words "I love you." At first I thought someone around me was talking, but I realized no one was. God was speaking directly to me. Wow! Being blessed with this experience has given me a security in life that no money or other material item could ever compare to. This experience has fortified me and I return to this moment often, re-living the experience.

Thank you Prophet for taking me to this glorious ocean where I was blessed to hear God tell me "I love you." People have always told me that God loves me, but hearing and experiencing it for myself made me understand the truth in this statement. God truly does love me. Really knowing this has forever changed me.

Written by Emily Allred

69

Visit Kingdom of Heaven Upon Wings of a Song

HU is the original creative Sound of God, which emanates from the Abode of God - the twelfth Heaven. From this sound vibration all other sounds originate. You can hear HU in the wind, in the passing of a plane in the sky above, in the flow of a creek - it is in everything. HU can also be sung in loving gratitude as a love song to God, which helps raise you up and open you up to God's Love and guidance. The Prophet, who is adept at spiritual travel, can guide Soul back to the birthplace of HU by traveling on the returning wave.

I vividly recall an evening some years ago during a retreat at the Nature Awareness School, when several friends and I sat with our teacher, Del Hall, upon some cut logs arranged in a circle outside a log cabin. As we sat in this circle, listening to the gentle sounds of a mountain evening, we began to sing HU, a love song to God. After some time I became aware of more sound than what the few of us were producing with our own voices. What I heard was HU, but it was richer, fuller, and deeper than the voice of our little group.

I became aware of a great beam of love, light, and sound that came down into the center of our circle, but what I noticed most at this time was the sound. This Divine Music seemed to come to me on a beam of love and sound meant just for me, as well as the larger beam that filled our circle. I gently felt the sound ringing peacefully through my head, as if it went straight from God, and through both my ears. This might seem like a rather odd picture, a man with the Light and Sound of God beaming right through his head, yet this was what I experienced. Perhaps the humor of this image helped to open my heart more, so I could accept even more of the Divine Love available in that moment.

Experiencing and hearing the HU in this way, I was aware that I was swiftly moving away from my body, and the circle of log benches. Upwards along this beam of sound I swiftly rose along with my friends and our teacher. Rather like a bead sliding along the rope of a necklace, or an old-time fireman sliding down the firehouse pole, we seemed to move quickly and effortlessly along this wave of sound. At some point I knew that we had arrived at our destination, and I felt both reverence and deep peace as I realized we were in a high and pure part of Heaven, the twelfth Heaven, a place from which love and mercy flows.

Here the sound of HU enveloped me, coming from every corner of my surroundings, and bringing with it joy, life, love, a sense of being welcomed home, and a peace so deep it cannot be described in words. This love song to God was now ringing out as a song of love from God, creating and sustaining life. And so, in a beautiful reality far beyond my imagination, a Prophet of God took me to the very doorstep of God upon a wave of sound.

Written by Timothy Donley

70

God Touched My Heart

You are loved by God and one of His desires is for you to know and live in this love daily. With the Prophet as your guide you can spiritually travel into the Heavens and experience this love from an aspect of the Divine for yourself - before the end of this physical life. Many who have been blessed to experience God's Love directly have one thing in common - they desire for you to experience it as well.

While I was deep in contemplation I was blessed with an amazing experience of Divine Love. It was given to me after singing HU, an ancient name for God, for a good length of time. As I sat with my physical eyes closed, my attention on the inner reality within me, I was aware of my spiritual teacher who I know as the Prophet, right beside me. He guided the real eternal me, Soul, higher and higher through world upon world of God's creation, the house of many mansions that Jesus spoke of two thousand years ago. The Prophet took me all the way home to the Abode of God Himself. I can best describe it as an expanse of God's Love and Mercy, one so vast that it was like a boundless ocean.

To be allowed to consciously return to my true home where God created me as Soul was a profound gift in and of itself. Yet God always has more love to give, for amid the ocean waves of God's Love, there appeared the Lord Himself in a form that I could relate to, one more personal than the boundless ocean. The Lord placed His hand on my heart and held it there. His eternal love poured into me and I knew beyond any shadow of a doubt that God truly loves me and has always loved me. Without conditions and without judgments He loves me. It is a love that has no beginning and no end. During that moment I knew that His Love is eternal and that it is personal, for God knows me and loves me just as much as any other part of His creation, and He loves me just as I am. I did not earn this gift but I was blessed to be able to receive it by the Grace of the Lord.

In the years since this Divine blessing of blessings there have been many times when I have not felt as loved as I did during that moment in eternity. Love is more than a feeling, for when I remember this blessing of standing before God as He touched me, I know that whether or not I feel loved, God loves me, and that all is well as I walk in His Love. This gift of God touching my heart, for which I thank the Prophet, the one whom God has ordained to take Soul home to Him, is a blessing that was not given to me just for my own benefit, or to be hoarded selfishly like a prized possession. This gift of Divine Love has blessed me with a greater capacity to give and receive love. It has helped to liberate me from selfish desires and to think more of the needs of others and to be able to truly hear and know in my heart what God, through His Prophet, is asking me to do. I also know that the love was given to me so that I can testify to this: God is real and God loves you.

Written by Roland Vonder Muhll

71

I am Soul, Light and Sound of God

There are certain "Core Truths" we teach at our retreats. Not only are they taught, folks actually get to experience them. One of the most important of these truths is "You do not have a Soul" rather, "You are Soul." This seemingly simple switch in perspective can set you free.

Many years ago, my father and spiritual teacher the Prophet, shared a simple yet profound Divine truth with me and a class of students at the Nature Awareness School. He shared with the group that we are Soul that has a body. Not what we had commonly thought - that we are a human body that has a Soul. He went on to give an example that it would be like identifying with ourselves as our cars - not as the driver, the animator, on the inside. Our "cars" will wear out over time but the real "us" will carry on and can get new "cars" for the next leg of our spiritual journey.

This simple, yet profound truth lifted a veil of illusion and opened the doors for so many wonderful possibilities and opportunities. Hearing and knowing that we are Soul meant that we are eternal. We are a Divine spark of God. We are children of God, created out of the Light and Sound of God and our potential for spiritual freedom, growth, and love is infinite.

Our bodies are a gift from God, to be respected and cared for, but it is not who we are, nor does it limit our connection with the Divine. As Soul we can be taught by an inner and outer spiritual guide. Together with our guide we are free to explore God's amazing inner Worlds, the various Heavens, in dreams and contemplations.

In one such contemplation, after singing HU, I found myself as Soul with my spiritual guide on an inner plane. We were on the beach at a vast and beautiful ocean. The golden light from the sun was shining down on us - it was warm and comforting. It bathed us in waves of love, peace, joy, security, and more. It was the Divine Light of God. The freedom and boundlessness of experiencing a moment purely as Soul is something that was never possible in my human body. I was able to feel absolute stillness and activity all at once and an indescribable strength in experiencing the real me. I felt free from the weight of the world and loved by God beyond my wildest imagination.

Our true home as Soul is the Heart of God. Thinking about that reality consciously reminds me who I really am at my core and brings with it so much peace. I may have a challenging day at work but knowing that I am Soul and not alone keeps a "bigger picture" and the "eternal view" present in my mind and heart. The events in daily life are less able to consume me when kept in perspective. As Soul I know that God has prepared me with everything I will ever need for my spiritual journey.

When I heard my father say, "I am Soul" I knew what I was hearing was truth. Over many years and through many experiences the truth revealed that night has sunk in deeper and deeper. The Divine has blessed me with personal experiences that solidified the knowingness in my heart. Even still, I know there is so much more to discover regarding the truth that we are Soul.

Written by Catherine Hughes

72

A Moment in Eternity

You are more than your physical body - you are Soul, a spiritual being. With the Prophet's help Soul is capable of leaving the physical and traveling into the Heavens. These journeys help one to gain in wisdom, love and understanding.

During a class at the Nature Awareness School Del led us on a guided contemplation to the high, Heavenly worlds. I have gone back to this particular experience many times to re-experience it. Though the core of the experience remains the same, each visit is different as I see things from a different perspective.

I was on the beach of a beautiful ocean and offered an opportunity to see an aspect of God. The Prophet pointed me to a golden path that lay before me along the beach. I ran down the path as it twisted and turned through the dunes. I arrived at a huge beam of light, the Light of God.

I stepped inside and realized that it did not seem bright. I knew I was within a beam of light, but could not see a distinction between the beam and everything else. In this place, there was not light and dark, high and low, or good and evil as it was beyond duality, beyond anything negative. I could not see the edge of the light because everything was light; there were no shadows. The light filled me with God's Love, saturating every part of me and more.

I rose up within the light, moving toward its source. I found myself within the Hand of God, gazing up into the Face of God. It seemed like a moment, yet each time I returned I found that I never left. Like there are no shadows there, it is beyond the restrictions of time and space. That moment is as real, vibrant, and present today as it was when I first experienced it. With the Prophet's help, I can savor that moment for a lifetime and continue to learn from it as I see things from different angles. In that moment gazing into the Face of God, I wanted for nothing. In that hand is where I have always been and shall be, in that moment in eternity.

Written by Jean Enzbrenner

73

A Drop of God's Love

There is no limit to what even a single drop of God's Love can do. It can move mountains, part seas, change destinies, heal relationships, and so much more. It is possible for you to visit the source and drink from this well.

I have learned by experience that it is entirely possible to perceive some of the wonders of God's Heavens while still walking the Earth. My body cannot visit these realms of God, but I, Soul, can do so with the help of my spiritual guide and teacher. He can and does take me on journeys beyond the confines of space and time even while my body sits upon the ground, or in a favorite chair.

After singing HU, an ancient love song to God, for quite some time, I had the opportunity to go on one such journey. I was led to what seemed like a vast ocean. What appeared at first to be water was actually unlimited quantities of love and mercy. Kneeling before this vast ocean of love and mercy, I knew that I was in the Presence of God, the creator of all things. The waters, and even what seemed to be the sands of the beach, were alive, energetic, glittering gold, sometimes blue with hints of other colors. There I experienced a deep peace and contentment, a sense of completeness far beyond what I had previously known. The living waters gently caressed me, like the hand of a father welcoming home a child who has been gone a long time.

Del, my teacher, suggested I dip one finger in this ocean and consider how much of God's Love is contained in a single drop. I was asked to consider how much impact a single drop of this Divine Love could have upon this Earth.

So I dipped my finger in this Heavenly Sea, and I experienced the living water glowing gold, tinged with other rich colors. It flowed around my finger, not as though pulled by gravity, but with loving intent and creative purpose, glowing intensely and spreading a strong but gentle warmth through my finger and entire being. Suddenly my consciousness expanded to see some of the potential of that little bit of Divine essence. In an instant I saw that this little drop of

God's Love could heal countless broken hearts and comfort countless hurting Souls. It can change the course of one's destiny, averting tragedy and bringing peace instead. There are no limits to what God's Love can do, though we may limit it with what our minds believe to be impossible.

So, dear reader, I testify to you that there is even now a Prophet of God who may take you to this same Divine well, that you may also experience and drink deeply of these living waters. God is real, and God's Love is available to you in quantities beyond measure. Drink deeply of God's Love, and share the peace and joy you find in this with those you love and meet. Thank you for the privilege of allowing me to share my experience with you.

Written by Timothy Donley

74

A Hug Filled With Gods Love

Love is the glue of the universe; it is the eternal all-creative power that holds everything together. It is God's Love for Soul that gives us life. It is our love for each other that inspires acts of kindness and sacrifice. For the serious seeker, becoming more adept at giving and receiving love is a must. Fortunately, most every experience we have in life can help us with this. Although it is our journeys into the Heavens where we can really grow in love.

I remember it like it was yesterday. We were in class, at the Nature Awareness School, and the Prophet of our times, Del Hall, offered us the opportunity to spiritually travel as Soul to one of God's many spiritual Temples. He guided us out of our physical bodies, as Soul, and escorted us to the temple. I was the last to arrive, and as I did I saw everyone standing on the stairs patiently waiting.

Just then the grand doors slowly began to open. A great white light shown through; it was so intense yet I did not have to shield my eyes from it. I could feel the love and comfort flowing out through the light, it was so inviting. Then a figure appeared in the doorway, the temple guardian. A tall thin man with a white beard dressed in a hooded white robe. I could see his eyes from a distance as they looked into me with love. He motioned to me. The Prophet and I climbed the stairs to meet him. As we approached he spoke no audible words yet I heard him welcome us. He took my hand and led me into a beautiful rotunda.

This was the most beautiful place that I had ever seen. As I looked around in awe he caught my eye and I heard "look up." I followed his gaze and saw the most amazing blue light emanating from the many windows that encompassed this enormous room. The blue light seemed to be alive; it had no physical source that I could see; yet it seemed to move in and around everything. Inside the temple there were no shadows, only light. The guardian in the robe again took me by the hand and looked deeply into me. His gaze was strong and full of love. He gave me a gift as the Prophet and I were getting ready to leave. He gave me a hug, something so simple yet so amazing. It was full of everything that I could ever need. I was filled with love, comfort, confidence, and the list goes on.

God knows exactly what we need when we need it. I thanked the gentleman and the Prophet for the amazing experience and we walked to the door. I stopped briefly to turn and look at that light one more time before we left. AMAZING! Since I arrived at the Nature Awareness School my life has been blessed. I am so grateful to have been able to experience Gods Love and Light in this truly awesome temple. Thank you, Prophet, for being my spiritual guide both on the inner and the outer.

Written by Anthony Allred

75

Staircase in Heaven

The experience others have had on their journey home to God can certainly inspire us. This is part of why we are now sharing some of the profound blessings and truths we have experienced. Still, it is through personal experience that God's truths can be fully known. This is one of the reasons the Prophet leads seekers into the Heavenly worlds to receive their own realizations.

I was participating in a class at the Nature Awareness School. We had just been singing HU. I was taken by the Prophet to one of the high Heavens in the Worlds of God. I knelt at the edge of a vast ocean. It appeared as a warm summer evening and all was deeply peaceful and still. I heard the Prophet say to explore the ocean and that I could ask for help to know what to do. I asked the Prophet, "What is in my heart?"

I wanted to be with God. "Where was God?" I wondered. I looked up to see a glowing white staircase appear over the water. I took a few steps up and then knelt. Some of the steps were wider than others. The Prophet urged me to go on. I took a few more steps then I knelt and felt within. Looking up I saw the staircase stretch as far as I could see and I knew it had no end.

Then a realization burst upon me. God was not in some far away destination. I was with God now; in this moment and every moment! No matter which step on the journey, God is with me. What a glorious truth to know in my heart!

In my daily life this truth helps me to relax. I know that no matter what is going on I am exactly where I need to be and God is with me.

Written by Carmen Snodgrass

76

I Am Soul

One of the most critical understandings the Prophet helps seekers come to is this: you do not "have" a Soul, rather, you "are" Soul - you "have" a body. At first this is merely a concept, but as you experience it for yourself in ever-greater capacities, it will truly set you free. In many ways this one truth is the gateway to almost boundless spiritual experiences and consciousness.

While participating in a guided spiritual exercise at the Nature Awareness School I was given an experience that combined with many previous ones to transform a concept I had to a deeper understanding. Often when we are being taught something new it starts as a concept that grows into a reality as we have personal experiences with what we are being shown.

What comes to mind as an example is when I learned how to ride a bike. I remember seeing others riding around the neighborhood balanced on two wheels and thinking it was a most marvelous adventure and that I wanted to be a part of it. I watched and studied how they got up on the bike, immediately began to pedal, then went soaring down the street. No problem. I had experience on the small bike that my father had taught me how to ride by running along and steadying me when needed.

With days of solo time I felt I was ready to move up to the next level. I begged to borrow one of the older boys' bike assuring him that I knew what I was doing, jumped up on it, reached down with my foot to spin the petals but was soon made aware that the bike was too big and my legs were too short. First try, crash. As the skin grew back on my hands my thought was that it must have been an equipment problem so I went searching for a different bike. I then began to notice that the design difference between a boy's bike and a girl's bike would allow me to reach the pedals in spite of my lack of leg length. The potential threat of ridicule of riding a girl's bike was, in my mind, off set by this being an experiment whose outcome was to have the ability to eventually soar like the older boys. Fortunately a girl in the neighborhood had such a bike and was kind enough to lend it to me if I promised to make the necessary repairs after I wrecked it; what a pessimist. No problem.

I jumped up on the bike and began to pedal down the street magically on two wheels at a rapid rate of speed tasting my new found freedom of being able to journey to neighborhoods I had never been, to see and do things in one afternoon that I had only dreamed of, expanding horizons before me....until I hit the parked car. Turning and stopping effectively didn't happen as easily as I thought it would. Second try, crash. Because of the damage to the car's tail light, the neighbor girl's bike, and my bloodied face, my father was now involved. In hindsight it was a blessing that saved me from myself. All the allowance money that I had to my name and all future earnings for quite some time went to providing restitution for the damage I caused.

My parents gave me an appropriately sized bike for my next birthday with my father teaching me how to properly ride a bike in the evenings after he came home from work. Because of his insights, instructional abilities, the faith he had in me, and the experience I had from the previous wrecks, I was soon soaring down the road. The concept of riding a bike had become a reality that grew to levels I would never have imagined. Riding at break neck speeds through the woods, going on long day trips, jumping off ramps, towing skaters behind with a rope, and eventually evolving to riding dirt bikes and cruising motorcycles. Such joy and freedom were found in the reality of riding a bike.

When my spiritual instruction began at the Nature Awareness School one of the basic tenets I was taught is that we are Soul. We don't have a Soul but are Soul with a physical body. When going home one day after having attended a weekend spiritual retreat I saw a bumper sticker stating that we are spiritual beings having a physical experience. Seeing it stated in another form allowed me to better understand it. Throughout the years during spiritual exercises I have been shown by the Prophet the limitlessness of Soul. I have been taken to spiritual temples, met spiritual masters, and been before the Light of God. Throughout my day I know a communication with the Prophet that is received in my heart, as Soul, which guides me in all aspects of my life. Like learning to ride a bike the concept was growing into a reality.

During the spiritual experience I mentioned in the beginning, the Prophet took us to the Abode of God. We began by singing HU, a love song to God. I soon became aware that I was kneeling on a golden beach facing an ocean of the most beautiful waters that were gently lapping at my knees. I was a light body, Soul, without physical limitations. Up and down the beach were other light bodies kneeling on the sand, some I knew as fellow students, all I knew were guided here by the Prophet.

On the horizon was the Light of God expanding towards us. During previous experiences the light had grown into an intensity that is beyond words that flowed into me cleansing and filling every recess of my being. This time the light was softer as if I was seeing it from beside the source of the light. Imagine what it is like to have a strong light shone on you; it is intense and it is all you can see. Now imagine how it would be to stand by the source of the light; it would be more diffused and illuminate all it was shined on. Coming across the ocean with the light was a sound, a vibration, the music of the Love of God that was expanding into all creation. I was reminded of the words of a great spiritual master: "The Light and Sound was of a wondrous whiteness like falling snow..." This one more experience expanded, deepened my knowingness of truly existing as Soul. Only as Soul could I have known the Light of God, the Love of God, in this form and magnitude. Only as Soul could I have known God's Light and Sound as one of the masters does. God so loves me that he stood me by his side and guided me to a deeper understanding. I am blessed, by His Grace, to have been given this gift. He knew exactly what I needed and when I was ready to more fully know my true self, Soul.

Like my father who wanted to show me how to properly ride a bike and open the possibilities of adventure for me, Our Heavenly Father wants us to know that we are Soul, a Divine being that he loves completely. When the truth that we are Soul grows from concept to reality, worlds of awareness are open to us and our spiritual growth is limitless. Accept the Prophet as your teacher and you will experience the joy and freedom of knowing your true self. I AM SOUL, YOU ARE SOUL.

Written by Terry Kisner

77

God and I Trust Him

It seems that mankind is always at least one dispensation behind God's timing and plan. What would it be like to accept spiritual guidance from the CURRENT Prophet sent by God rather than total reliance on a former Prophet who can no longer teach in the physical? Perhaps the following testimony can answer the above question for the reader.

In the Bible, John 14:26, Jesus says that the Father will send us a Comforter in his name and that He will teach us all things, and bring us remembrance. This promise ensures us that we will not be alone, that we will always have a guide to help us find our way back to our true home in the Heart of God.

During a spiritual retreat at the Nature Awareness School, Del Hall, who is the current Prophet of our times, led us in a guided spiritual experience. As the Prophet he has the special ability to teach and guide us both in the physical and in the spiritual worlds as well. He does this as a direct representative of God. This gift is available for all of us, from God. The Prophet has helped me to manifest more of God's Love and blessings into my daily life.

We started by singing HU for quite some time. HU is a pure love song to God, and is a powerful way for us to draw nigh to God, and to rise above the gravity of our life down here, to be able to experience God and all of His glory and love more fully and unobstructed. After singing HU, Del guided us through an experience that continues to bless me to this day. In Spirit, he took me all the way home to the Abode of God! I found myself before a vast Ocean of God's Light. I could do nothing but kneel in extreme reverence for God's glory and splendor that was before me. Not out of fear, but out of intense love for God. God Himself then filled me with blazing white light, poured directly into my heart. This Light of God contained an abundance of life giving blessings. Love, peace, nourishment, healings, anything I could possibly ever need but not even know to ask. I accepted as much as I could possibly take. This love transformed me from the inside out. I felt alive and like my true self more than ever before. Words cannot describe the level of deep peace that I felt. In that moment, everything felt complete and right. There was not a single thing that I lacked or needed. This blessed me immensely in that moment, and also continues to nourish and sustain me.

The Prophet then brought me, as Soul, to my physical apartment on Earth. He showed me that God's Love was already woven in to all aspects of my life. He reminded me that the fabric that makes up all things in my home and life are actually the Love of God. This new perspective helps me to be more grateful for the countless ways God blesses me in life. I now recognize more of the beautiful gifts from God that have been there all along, that I may not have recognized. The Prophet then took me to my place of work, and showed me that God's Love is already there as well. He even helped me to add more of God's Love. Being at my job since then, I often have remembrance of this experience and it continues to open my heart, and remind me how much God loves me. Knowing that the Prophet has blessed my workplace to allow more of God's Love to fill it is a huge gift that helps me when I need a little extra boost. The seemingly simple act of remembrance allows God's Love to manifest more fully into my daily life, and allows this experience to live on and as it continues to bless me.

There are so many people in the world who crave deeply to have a real, personal, and intimate experience with God. Just once could change their life forever. If I could pass along one thing, it's that this absolutely is possible in this life! One does not have to wait until they die to experience God and all of His glory and splendor. We can experience Heaven a little bit at a time while still living down here. I'm blessed to have been led many times through the high spiritual realms, all of the way home to the Heart of God. It requires a very high level guide to get you there. This guide is the Prophet of our times, fully authorized by and backed by God to help lead His children home to him. Del Hall is the one who God has bestowed His mantle on. The power is in the Light and Sound of God, or the Holy Spirit that God allows to work through him. Much like how the Prophets of the Bible wore a special mantle of God's power and Love to help seekers link up with God back then. God is a living God and has not abandoned us. It is untrue to think that God would not continue to send us Prophets to help guide us home to Him.

In the Bible, Jesus promised us a Comforter, and that promise will always be fulfilled.

Written By Sam Kempf

78

Thousand Fold Answer to a Prayer

God hears the prayers of our hearts. He hears our cry for comfort and sees our outstretched hands. When the time is right our prayers will be answered, usually greater than we could have ever imagined.

As a little girl growing up, I went to Sunday school, where I especially loved to sing the song, "Jesus Loves Me." I sang it in my little girl voice, "Jesus loves me this I know, for the Bible tells me so..."

I knew God loved me, for the Bible said so, but God and Jesus seemed so far away. As I grew older, like a small seed inside me, a yearning for God began to grow. It sprouted and grew, and by the time I was about fourteen or fifteen years old, while I was listening to a Neil Diamond song, I knew and voiced the prayer in my heart. I was alone in our basement, listening to the Neil Diamond song "Brother Love's Traveling Salvation Show." When Neil said, "Take your hand and put it out to the man up there; that's what he is there for," I looked up, I reached my hand up as high as I could reach, and I looked up to Him. I couldn't see Him, I couldn't sense Him, I couldn't touch Him, but I knew that He was out there, and I so wanted God to take my hand as I reached up to Him. With tears streaming down my face, I begged to God as I sang along, "Take my hand dear Lord, walk with me this day, in my heart I know, I will never stray…"

I grew up and had forgotten about this experience, though I still had a deep yearning inside of me. I began going to the Nature Awareness School where Del taught us how to listen to God's communication with us. He taught us to sing HU, a love song to God. Singing HU is a beautiful way to express our love to God, and it helps us to listen to Him better. One day Del led us in contemplation where he, the Prophet, took us to God's Ocean. It was an immense ocean of love that went on forever. I found myself kneeling in reverence in the soft sand at the water's edge with the Prophet beside me.

It was very peaceful, with tiny waves lapping at the sand. I looked up and saw God looking at me with an immense amount of love in His eyes. I saw His hand reaching out to me. I stretched up my hand towards God's with all of my being. I so wanted to touch Him. As God gently touched my finger, brilliant white light that felt like love, flowed through my hand, down my arm, and filled my whole being. More and more light and love flowed into me as I took in all that I could. After it stopped, I found myself still kneeling in the sand, though I was changed forever. God had reached down, touched my hand, and filled me with His Love, and transformed me in a way that words cannot describe. I looked up and saw the Prophet beside me. I was so grateful to him for bringing me to God's Ocean, making this amazing experience possible.

After this experience I remembered my deep prayer and reaching out for God many years ago. My prayer was answered in a way that was so much more than I could have imagined. It was made possible by God's Prophet. Only a true Prophet of God can take you safely into the inner worlds. The Prophet is the way; the Prophet is the only way to God. As Jesus said, "I am the way, the truth, and the life: no man cometh unto the Father but by me," God's current Prophet now is the way. God loves us so much that he always has a Prophet on Earth to lead us to Him. Through my love for the Prophet, he took my hand, and he brought me face to face with God. Wow.

Written by Diane Kempf

79

The Light and the Way

To experience God's Light, in any form or color, is a gift of love from God. It is through His Light that God delivers His many blessings to Soul. Specifically though, when God's Light comes in the form of golden light - it is one way for God to directly say "I Love you." This love from God can melt away the walls we have built through our lifetimes and replace them with true comfort and protection. The Prophet shows us the way to directly experience the Light and Love of God.

After singing HU, I enjoy spending time in silence. In those moments of silence in tune with the Divine, insights often come. I do not expect anything, though I may begin the HU with an intent or question. In this HU, I expected only to express my love to God but I received a beautiful gift in return.

We sang a long HU one evening at the Nature Awareness School. After the HU, I saw a brilliant gold light that enveloped me. This light was all there was and it was everything. I could hear ocean waves and feel their rhythm, but everything I saw was golden light. I knew that this was God, specifically God's Love. I accepted and felt cradled in God's Love, rocked like a child by golden light.

Then the Prophet stood before me in the center of the light. I took his hands and he said, "I am the light and the way." I stepped into him. I felt relief as if a great burden had been removed. This surprised me since I had not felt burdened before. After a moment, I saw what it was. Within the Prophet, I was safe from everything from which I had ever tried to protect myself. The dangers were not physical, but those created in my mind. I had shed armor intended to protect against what others may think of me, mistakes I might make, and from disappointing loved ones or even God.

Instead of armor, the Prophet's love and acceptance now surrounded and supported me. I felt more my true self than I ever have before. I was free to be myself and even to make mistakes, which were not to be feared, but accepted as a gift from which to learn and grow.

While I know this experience was real and true, I also know that I must nurture it. I am responsible for remembering the experience and for staying close to the Prophet, especially if I feel any of the old armor returning. The Prophet's light healed me, but it is following His way that will make the healing last.

Written by Jean Enzbrenner

80

The Touch of God

How do you write a worthy introduction to a testimony about traveling spiritually with the Prophet home to Heaven, being ordained by God at a vast ocean of light and love, and then sent forth to help others experience this for themselves? I've been looking it over quite some time now, for an answer to that very question and I keep coming back to simply - wow! Please hear the truth in the following statement; everything in your wildest imagination about what your relationship with God could be, the deepest desires of your heart, and the dreams you hold dear - they are all truly possible.

There was once a time in my life when I wondered if God was real. I wondered if Heaven was a real place, and if there was more to life. I read how Paul of the New Testament told of a person who "was caught up to the third Heaven," and I wondered just how many Heavens there could be. I have been blessed with many experiences that began to answer these questions and more. Each of these experiences, which have been given to me on my journey so far, have been profound. Yet there are some, which are not only profound, but pivotal. This is one of those experiences.

During a retreat at the Nature Awareness School several years ago, I sang HU, a love song to God with many friends, and with our teacher Del Hall. We sang HU for a long time, and as we sang, I was keenly aware of a bright blue light, which grew brighter and stronger as we sang. We also lovingly sang the names of some other teachers, some Prophets who have helped us at different points in our lives. With my eyes closed, I perceived other colors of light as well. For a time we seemed to be suspended in a rich violet light which surrounded all of us. I realized that this was the color of the Heaven we were passing through. All at once, a blue whirlwind of light embraced us and it seemed that we spiraled upwards. In my heart I knew that this blue light was from the Prophet of God, our guide on this amazing and sacred journey. The violet glow gave way to a brilliant gold, and then a stunning white light of unimaginable brightness filled my view. I am not sure if the light faded some, or if I adjusted to its brilliance, but a great peace came over me as I found myself kneeling with gratitude and reverence on the shores of a great ocean. It was clear that I did not come there on my own, or by accident, but was brought there by the Prophet, who I perceived was kneeling next to me as a living example of the deepest reverence. I had been brought here before, but this time would be different. This was no ordinary ocean. As I looked out over it, it seemed vaster than all the oceans of Earth, and what had at first looked like water now sparkled and glowed, alive with love and creative energy. I could see that I was made of the same love and light, which surrounded me in the choppy waves, and the sands of the beach responded to my touch with great love and tenderness, like a loving parent welcoming a child who has been gone a long time. I had heard tales and songs of living waters, yet now I was surrounded by them, experiencing this vast ocean filled with love, mercy, light, and the sound of HU. I felt at home, so deeply at home that I had no desire to ever leave the majesty of this place. I was in the Presence of God, caught up in the twelfth Heaven. In this wondrous place, which these words cannot begin to describe, the living waters, the embracing sands, the brilliance of many suns, the horizon and what seemed to be sky above were all aspects of God, the creator of all things.

All at once the waters calmed. This white-blue ocean came to rest as the living waves gave way to a perfect smoothness, like a single facet of a blue diamond that went on forever in all directions. With deep gratitude for the blessing of this experience, and with an overwhelming reverence, I looked deep into the ocean, still kneeling. As I looked into the endless, light-filled depths of love and mercy, I was asked to place my right index finger upwards, up over this Divine Ocean. Out of this perfect stillness a great figure arose, the figure of a man yet more than a man, shining with brilliant white and gold light. I was mainly aware of his hand, a great golden hand, the very Hand of God. From the very tip of this great finger a massive, searing beam of white and golden light shot forth to my own finger. I could perceive that others were also experiencing the same. Divine Love, appearing as a great light more intense than I could imagine, shot forth and filled my entire being. My own finger burned white hot with a great intensity, yet without pain. It seemed as though all time and space had collapsed or disappeared for an instant, and everything I ever was and ever shall be was contained in that moment. For this brief but massive moment of eternity my entire world was simply me, and the Lord my God. In a flash, a thought came to mind: I wondered if Michelangelo had been witness to such an event before he painted the ceiling of the Sistine Chapel. His painting of God reaching out to Adam seemed to represent what I was now experiencing.

Thus filled with a great stream of Divine Light, Love, peace, joy, and more, I lacked nothing, yet I was not sure how long I could survive such an experience. The Lord our God was providing us all with what was needed to begin helping others find what we have been given. We were being ordained to share God's Light and Love with so many others, including you, dear reader.

As the experience continued, I stretched to accept even more of this download of love, and finally, when I almost felt I could take no more, the experience changed. I lowered my hand, my finger glowing white, and placed it in the living waters of the ocean. As I and my friends did so, some of the love we had been given shot out across the waters like lines of fire, converging, and splitting out into smaller lines. Great waves formed on the ocean and swept across it. In my

Soul body, at this great ocean, I lay down to rest in the living sands, at the Abode of God. The Prophet inwardly comforted me and others, helping us to retain our balance and accept the amazing gifts we had been given and I thanked him for taking me to God. It has taken me much longer than a single class to begin to understand this experience. And there is much more to it than what these simple words can describe. The gifts we had been given were not only for us, but for you as well, and for you to pass on to others. As the light given from God to us shot out across the ocean, splitting into many directions, so it is that we now share some of what we have been given with many around the world. At the time I was sure this was my first such experience, yet I have since discovered that it was neither my first nor my last. Yet an experience in the higher Heavens is not an experience in time, so with the aid of the Prophet, it may be returned to as a living experience, rather than the sort of static memory to which we have become accustomed. Someone who has had such an experience is endowed with the ability to be of greater service to other children of God.

And so it is that when the seeker of God has returned home and found what he has desired to find, he may be given an opportunity to go forth again, and share the Light he has received from God in a manner harmonious with his own personality and approach to life. As one journey is completed, another begins, even more amazing than the first.

Written by Timothy Donley

The Nature Awareness School

Del Hall and his wife Lynne established the Nature Awareness School in 1990. They continue to facilitate spiritual retreats at the school located in the Blue Ridge Mountains near Love, Virginia. Del is a graduate of the United States Naval Academy and has a Master of Science Degree from the University of West Florida. He was a Navy Fighter Pilot and Jet Flight Instructor.

Although Del has a technical background his passion is in helping other Souls recognize their Divine Nature and the ways of God. Del has facilitated hundreds of spiritual retreats. During these retreats the Voice of God has responded in magnificent and life improving ways.

On July 7th, 1999, after years of service and intense spiritual training in the ways of God, Del attained spiritual mastership. His position was upgraded on October 22nd, 2012 when God ordained him to be His Prophet.

Del has learned to follow Divine guidance to the benefit of all who are open to personal growth. He teaches them how to have their own experiences with the Divine while fully conscious.

Del then helps with the understanding and integrating of these experiences into daily life. Abundance follows.

Del's son joined the school as an instructor after fifteen years of in-class training to develop and lead the Dream Study Retreats. Del IV also lives on the school property in the beautiful Blue Ridge Mountains with his family. He is a nationally exhibited artist who attended the School of the Museum of Fine Arts in Boston and has paintings in over seventy-five public and private collections.

During the Dream Study Retreats Del IV teaches people about the rich history of dream study and how to better remember and understand their own day and night dreams. As an ancient source of Divine wisdom and guidance, dreams are available for those who make the effort to pay attention.

The off-site events division of the Nature Awareness School, "Uplift With Dreams," hosts Dream Study Workshops, HU sings, and accepts public speaking invitations around the country.

Contact Information

Nature Awareness School
P.O. Box 219
Lyndhurst, Virginia 22952

natureawarenessschool@gmail.com
(540) 377-6068

Visit **NatureAwarenessSchool.com** or

UpliftWithDreams.com
for retreat descriptions and schedule.

Weekly Inspiration

Nature Awareness School's online publication "Weekly Inspiration" contains many stories that show the Hand of God working miracles in people's lives. Stories include help with careers, health concerns, relationships, healing, daily guidance, day and night dreams, spiritual travel into the Heavens, and so much more. To sign up for free email notifications of new posts please visit WeeklyInspiration.com

Testimonies of God's Love – Book One

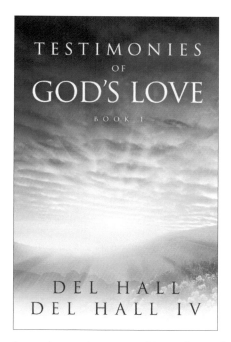

What if God is actively trying to communicate with you in order to bless all areas of your life but you do not know God's special language? God is a living God. He sends His Prophets to teach the "Language of the Divine" and to show His children the way home to their Father. Divine Love and guidance has always been and is still available to you. Learning how to listen, trust, and respond to this guidance will improve your life and bring more abundance to your heart.

Within these pages are miraculous modern day testimonies written by students of the Nature Awareness School. Here they learned how to recognize God's guiding hand in all areas of their lives. Through dreams, Divine insight, experiencing the Light and Sound of God directly, or traveling with an inner guide into the HEAVENS these true stories show us God is indeed alive and still communicating. These testimonies show how God is reaching out and desires to develop a more personal and loving relationship with each of us.

These testimonies will shatter any limitations to what is truly possible in your relationship with God. They show how others are experiencing God's Love and Grace and will serve as inspiration on your own journey home to the Heart of God.

Visit Loved Ones In Heaven

Have you ever lost a loved one and longed for just one more moment together? What if it were truly possible to have this time together? Could a visit, if even for a short moment of time, help heal your heart? Would knowing for certain that they still exist and are doing well bring you a deep peace? What if you could express your love once again? Imagine how that would feel!

Visiting loved ones in Heaven is possible! God can bless Souls separated by physical death by reuniting them spiritually for short visits. The authors of the testimonies in this book do not have to imagine what such a wonderful opportunity would be like. They each have experienced the profound blessings of such moments. They chose to share their experiences to praise the loving God that blessed them and to inspire you, the reader, to strengthen your own relationship with God. Within this book are spiritual tools and daily practices that may help YOU to have your OWN similar experiences.

These testimonies will shatter perceived limitations as to what is possible in your relationship with God and God's Prophet. Spiritually meeting departed parents, grandparents, aunts, uncles, children, close friends, and even beloved pets can heal broken hearts. These moments together also bless your loved one as they too desire to reach out to you. These beautiful and heartwarming stories are possible because God loves both you and your loved ones.

Testimonies of God's Love – Book Two

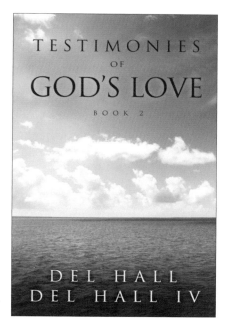

What if God is actively trying to communicate that He LOVES YOU, wants a personal relationship with YOU, and wants to bless all areas of YOUR life?

God's Love and guidance shine through every day in thousands of ways for those who know His language. He sends His Prophets to teach the "Language of the Divine" and to show His children the way home to their Father. Learning how to really see, listen, trust, and respond to this love and guidance will improve your life and bring more abundance to your heart.

Within these pages are miraculous modern day testimonies written by students of the Nature Awareness School. It is here they learned how to recognize God's Love and guiding hand in their lives.

Whether through dreams, Divine insight, experiencing the Light and Sound of God directly, or traveling with an inner guide into the HEAVENS, these real experiences show that God truly loves us. These testimonies illustrate how God is reaching out and desires to develop a more personal and loving relationship with each of us.

These testimonies will shatter any limitations as to what is truly possible in your relationship with God. They reveal how others are experiencing God's Love and Grace and will serve as inspiration on your own journey home to the Heart of God.